PRAISE FOR *Jennifer Rosen*

"I laughed. I cried. It was better than *Cats*."
~ Darryl Roberts, Publisher, *Wine X* magazine

"As always, witty and informative.
Pithy. You are such a talented writer!"
~ Bruce Cameron, Author; *8 Simple Rules for Dating
My Teenage Daughter*

"An amazing writer. I love these columns. Brilliantly written,
edgy viniferal-infused prose on the wine industry as we know it.
I'm a total fan."
~ Bob Guccione, Jr.

"Witty and entertaining.
I remain a devoted and admiring reader"
~ Allen Meadows / Burghound.com

"Terrific, very funny."
~ Leonardo Locascio / Winebow Imports

"Damn you're good"
~ Terry Theise / *Food & Wine* magazine's
2005 Importer of the Year

"Comic intent is clear; chock full of info as well.
And I love her penchant for bluntness—totally wacked.
Chotzi [Rosen] tackles lots of topics wine lovers care about,
and she does so with real zing."
~ Tish / Wine for All

"You write REALLY well. I'm very impressed. You are very funny!"
~ Jan Eliot / *Stone Soup Cartoons*

The Cork Jester's

GUIDE TO WINE

GUIDE TO WINE

An Entertaining Companion
For Tasting It, Ordering It & Enjoying It.

Jennifer Rosen

CLERISY PRESS

The Cork Jester's® Guide to Wine

COPYRIGHT © 2006 BY JENNIFER ROSEN

For further information, contact the publisher at

CLERISY PRESS
1700 MADISON ROAD
CINCINNATI, OH 45206

Edited by **ANGELA HOXSEY**

Cover and interior designed by **STEPHEN SULLIVAN**

Jester illustration by **KARI LEHR, BIRCH DESIGN STUDIOS**

Author photos :
© **FORD STOCKTON MCCLAVE**
DENVER, CO USA 303-394-3673

Distributed by **PUBLISHERS GROUP WEST**

PRINTED in the U. S. of A.
1   2   3   4   5   6   7   8   9   10

ACKNOWLEDGMENTS

I'd like to thank:

Nick Selvy, for research, list work and adding delight to my life.
Maria Cote and Mike Rudeen, my *Rocky Mountain News* editors, who kick
my procrastinating ass every week but never fire me.
Jessica Yerega, who helped wrangle a bunch of ornery columns into one corral.
Angela Hoxsey, editor extraordinaire, who knows wine as well as words.
Eric Orange of Localwineevents.com, for delivering readers, plus he's always
bugging me to push his site in print so maybe this will shut him up.
Richard Hunt, for plucking me out of the self-publishing ghetto and making
an honest writer of me.
Lane Steinberg, for his hallucinogenic haiku.
Monty Jorgensen, whose fabulous website design nets me ten marriage
proposals a day.
Marilyn Ross, for inspiration, organization and a terrific contract.
Ted Dewald, who never misses a column and raises hell when I do.
Don Peters: Yo, Don, I said *court* jester. But don't ever get your hearing fixed.
Jean-Noël Fourmeaux, who handles what I'm hopeless at and is always there
for me, no matter how hard I make it.
Readers who email: I keep every word, praise or vitriol. You teach, energize
and inspire me. Don't ever stop!

And most of all:

To my father Blair
Who taught me:

You don't ever have to grow up and get serious.

Blair Chotzinoff
1926–2005
Play in Peace

Contents

8

11

Introduction

I'LL BE HONEST WITH YOU. I can't simplify wine. Frankly, wine is complicated, and gets more so every day. I can hardly keep up with all the new wineries and regions. Daily, people ask, "What do you think of the new Wasted Walrus Pinot Blanc?" And I have no idea what they're talking about.

But everyone insists wine is simple. "Don't worry about ratings," they say, "just drink what you like." But you're no dummy. You wouldn't order Blue Nun in front of the boss, no matter how much you loved it.

"Americans need to start viewing wine as an everyday beverage," claim producers. Then, on the back label they write, "Pairs well with truffled oxen snout in finnberry reduction on a bed of flaked Andalusian taro." Sure. Every Thursday.

The front label is even worse. But winemakers refuse to see the problem. "Reading a Moravian label is easy!" they say. "Just three quality levels, ten regions and four grapes. Anyone can learn that!" Yeah, anyone who plans to spend the rest of his life in Moravia.

They don't factor in learning those "simple rules" for all the countries on the planet. They don't realize that just locating the Moravian aisle at Wine-a-Rama can be a major expedition involving tents, compass and handheld GPS. (Safety note: Always inform a buddy before going in.)

Price is another bed of quicksand. Do big bucks guarantee quality, or just brand you as a sucker? How come that $200 Château Humpty-Dump left you cold, while your $6.99 Shiraz was delicious?

Even more slippery is that wine is a living creature. You never know what lurks under that cork. Many wines go through puberty, like adorable children morphing into repulsive, sullen adolescents. Pour that Riesling you adored in December today, and instead of exuberant fruit you get attitude: "Fine, you're going to pour me. Like I care."

Then there's wine talk; a tortured, arcane lingo that seems designed to keep you out of the club. You might well decide it's a bunch of pretentious mumbo jumbo for snobs, and you don't need it. Or you might become a snob, shoring up your shaky confidence with ratings, prices and exclusive allocations.

But there's another approach. Sure we all swig sometimes, but what separates wine from apple juice and root beer is the possibility of going so much deeper. You can discover chemistry, agriculture, marketing, politics, history, psychology and geology, all in one glass. Not to mention romance and passion. Wine lovers all speak of their First Time, a quasi-spiritual moment of awakening to wine's wonderment. After that, it's a life sentence. I've seen it happen to even the most confirmed beer sluggers.

Take Ted Dewald, a staunch suds man, ex-military and tough as nails. Despite reading my columns for years, he continues to cling proudly to his vintage-idiot status. All that vinous gobblety-gook is for touchy-feely artistes, not coarse Neanderthals such as him. Then, the other day, after a bottle of Petite Sirah, he writes me this:

Leave it to the damn French to call a 290-pound linebacker a pansy ass wide receiver. Why do they do that!? First thing I noticed was that it looked like red crude oil but it still poured like liquid. Not petite.

I stuffed my nose into the glass and it smelled very, very red but not especially menacing or heavy. A little dusty though, so I figured it was robust. Still, not anything petite about it.

Then I took a swig, held it a bit and the tannin was immediately apparent—as was the weight. Definitely NOT petite.

Then I swallowed. Zinfandel, Grenache: take a seat. The big dog has arrived. And it leaves some cotton to clean off the tongue...and the cheeks...and the lips. This ain't petite. This is definitely XXL, at least.

Some American should give this a manly name and it would reach a manly market. I bet a lot of women try it and never drink it again and men just won't try it. I'm thinking of putting it in a bottle labeled something like Bite Me or Serious Shit or Manly Red Wine or maybe just XXL.

I've had half a glass and I already feel it. You're right about the alcohol...

As far as I'm concerned, that's wine writing. He came, he tasted, he reacted. No fear. No notions of how it should be done. He'd hate to admit it, but he's clearly learned something over the years about tannins and grapes. But mostly he's learned to look wine squarely in the face.

Which is the most any of us can do. I could offer you a textbook crammed with facts to memorize. But why should you bother—you have Google. Besides, too much information is as bad as none. A wise winemaker told me, "Drinking wine with a sommelier is like making love to a gynecologist: it's better if they don't tell you everything they know."

Instead, I offer a series of bite-sized stories; Trojan horses filled with facts programmed to infiltrate and lodge in your brain, with no effort at all on your part. They're arranged to take you from vineyard to grape to bottle to glass to table to big, red stain on the carpet. But feel free to plunge in anywhere; like a mosaic, each tile can stand alone. I can't make wine simple. But I can make it fun and beautiful, instead of esoteric and intimidating. The minute you realize it's OK to stumble along like the rest of us, asking questions and paying attention to your own reactions, then you'll begin what I hope will be a lifelong love affair with wine.

In the Vineyard

"HERE AT CHÂTEAU CLICHÉ WE LISTEN TO THE GRAPES. A delicate balance of soil, sunshine, worms and magnetic fields nurtures their unique personalities. We at CC believe in minimal intervention; in letting our grapes express themselves and their terroir!"

I get that press release at least three times a day. Everyone, including giant, corporate factories, wants it clear that, "Our wine is made in the vineyard, not in giant, corporate factories."

Agriculture may not be your thing, but it's the holy-holy of wine these days. So let's find out what, exactly, is going on in those magical vineyards.

STRANGE BREW
Biodynamic: crazed cult?
Or crazed cult that makes good wine?

THE INTERVIEW WAS IN FRENCH, and mine was still at that fragile level where you don't want to let on that half the time you have no idea what the conversation is about. So when the winemaker started talking about stuffing cow horns with powdered quartz, burying them under a grove of 100-year-old oak trees from Easter to mid-September, and digging them up when the moon was full, I just kept nodding and writing, assuming I had lost something—my brain, perhaps—in translation.

16

In fact, he was explaining *biodynamics*. Just as, a few decades ago, mothers re-embraced breast-feeding after a half-century of sanitized formula, winemakers are now waking up to nature, exploring the advantages of returning Earth to its full and upright position.

Vineyard monoculture strips the ground, and organic farming replenishes it and keeps the soil aerated for good drainage. Some are going green to revitalize desiccated family vineyards. Some are sick of—and from—inhaling pesticides. Yet others start sustainable vineyards from scratch. Almost all report improved flavors and personality in the resulting wine.

But how green is your bottle? What do earthy label terms tell you?

Organic Grapes means grapes grown with no chemical pesticides or fertilizers. Wineries often plant cover crops like grains, salad greens or flowers between vine rows to conserve water, add nutrients and attract friendly bugs. Nasty ones are foiled by jamming their reproductive signals with synthetic pheromones. Instead of sweeps with the crop duster, natural fungicides are used sparingly, only where needed.

100 Percent Organic is stricter: no chemicals allowed in the winery, either. Alas, it's almost impossible to stabilize wine without adding sulfites, and there's little reason to try: they're not responsible for the headaches that consumers pin on them. Besides, sulfites are naturally present on grapes skins and are also a product of fermentation, so, added or not, all wines contain some.

Biodynamic is part viticulture, part cosmic weirdness. The farm is considered a self-sustaining system, where animals and their manure play an important role. You start with pulverized rock, because Earth and her minerals are living, breathing creatures. You mix it with eggshells and cow manure and pack it all into the horn of an organically fed, clean-living cow from the Pyrenees. (Cow horns and deer antlers capture the

17

earth's energies.) After burying and exhuming the stuff, you "dynamise" it by adding water, and in certain cases, dandelions, nettles and oak-bark, and spinning it in a centrifuge. The resulting tea is used to repel (never kill) pests and fungi, as well as to augment the soil. But before you apply it, you must consult the calendar.

Created forty years ago by a German named Maria Thun, the calendar has been translated into twenty-one languages and has sold over 100,000 copies. It's based on the premise that planets and constellations affect energy patterns on earth. Zodiac signs are associated with different areas of plant growth; therefore, if you grow carrots or potatoes, you plant on dates auspicious for roots. Fruits, flowers and leaves each have their times too.

Maria Thun didn't just come up with this stuff. She was a disciple of Austrian Rudolf Steiner, born in1891, founder of the Anthroposophy movement, dedicated to the forces of the spiritual world. He communicated telepathically with the voiceless residents of Atlantis, who happened to be Aryans, which was important, as his movement looked down on the mixing of races.

Anthroposophy, in turn, was a spin-off of Theosophy, which was big on reincarnation and purifying your soul. Theosophy enjoyed great popularity at the turn of the last century. Converts called each other "comrade," and went to a lot of meetings, both to fill the gaping spiritual void left in their lives by the impersonal industrialization of the modern world, and because there were donuts.

My grandfather, a young Russian immigrant in New York at the time, was initiated into the cult by enlightened friends. He tried his damnedest to purify body and soul and overcome worldly temptations. But you know how young guys are. He finally chucked the whole thing for the same reason Oscar Wilde quit socialism: it took too many evenings.

You can trace this pseudo-spiritual soup of séances, magnetism and phrenology back a lot further, but the striking thing is that its adherents make fabulous wine right alongside their organic and high-tech neighbors.

The surprising thing about biodynamics is who's doing it. Nicolas Joly of the Loire Valley fits the wacko picture. He credits the shape of a barrel with "life forces" and "enormous wisdom," and ferments his wine in buried, clay amphorae because "clay can cure; it is strongly linked to the sun." Others, like Michel Chapoutier of the Rhône, embrace much of the bio ethos, but think following all the details gets a bit silly. Prominent wineries all over Europe have jumped on board and are producing excellent wine. Go figure.

Most of the time, though, we don't even know we're drinking it. Lots of vineyards don't bother jumping through the hoops necessary to get the official stamp. Some want the chemical option as a safety net. Others think the free and natural ethos just doesn't jibe with the rigidity of certification.

Going native has its challenges. South America has it easiest. Their only bugaboo, the nematode, found its match in new, resistant rootstocks. They foil the root-louse phylloxera, scourge of vineyards worldwide, by regularly flooding their vineyards. But that's totally illegal in Europe. And European Mad Cow ministers have slapped a ban on the bovine body parts so important to bio preparations. Both Europe and California battle fungi and pests that cede only to copper spray, which is not on the organic menu.

To mainstream, American customers, "organic wine" still has the hippy-dippy smack of something made from peaches and filtered through a bong. Yet terms like natural, organic and biodynamics are quite the vogue in Europe; they're used to sell everything from diapers to Dolcetto. I imagine living on a tightly packed continent, where every feature of the landscape has been altered by man at some point or another in history, gives you a much more urgent impression of a dying planet in need of resuscitation.

The Save-the-Earth, recycling ethos is more vivid in Europe, where there's simply less Earth to go around and what's there has long since lost its virginity.

I once drove to Roswell, New Mexico with a French eco-warrior who was interested in aliens. We drove through places where there was nothing but grass between the car and horizon in every direction. We crossed painted deserts, mountain ranges and sand dunes, with only the paved road reminding us that other humans existed. After three days of this, he appeared to grasp the infinitesimal impact of his existence on the universe. If he didn't go home and commit suicide, at least I think he quit sorting glass from plastic.

ROCKET SCIENCE
Farming in the space age

THE ART OF VITICULTURE is an ancient one, requiring harmony with the earth, an intuitive sensitivity to the rhythms of nature and a NASA satellite. Yes, while primitive people still scratch the earth with sticks, bringing forth grapes and somehow coaxing them to ferment, larger wineries are turning to the aid of space-age science.

Of course, winemakers have always taken advantage of the newest technology. For eons, wine could only be stored in the cupped hands. We'd have evolved webbed fingers, had it not been for the invention of the cup, a critical breakthrough that freed up early man's hands for such tasks as hitting, scratching, and making rude gestures at the guy who invented the wheel.

Weather has always been crucial to grape growers. The ones who could predict an early spring frost or heavy rain during harvest had a definite leg up on the competition. Helped by such meteorological tools as cloud formations, self-conscious groundhogs and the relative thickness of the winter coat of the yak, vineyards have done a pretty good job over the years delivering grapes.

Variations in temperature, moisture, sunlight and soil on the tiniest plot of land—in short, microclimate—also make a huge difference in wine quality, as anyone knows who has tried to buy a bottle of Romanée-Conti (a four-acre vineyard in Burgundy) and had his mortgage request turned down. Generations of Old World winemakers have passed down knowledge of every inch of their property and how best to cultivate it.

New World wineries, on the other hand, have had to figure this stuff out by trial and error. This is dicey when you're selling futures on $75 bottles but you don't even know if you can grow Ripple. Not that a little old thing like quality would keep wineries from charging whatever price gullible consumers will swallow.

But now science has come to the rescue in the form of satellite imaging from NASA. To wrap your mind around this, it helps to understand something technical about satellites. For that information, I contacted esteemed science writer Steve Castle who explains, "Satellites work the same way as TV: They're magic. The only difference is they're up in space." That would explain why, since 1957, over 25,975 objects have been put into orbit, but only 8,733 remain there. It's obvious those other 17,243 objects account for acid rain, the hole in the ozone layer and why at the oddest moments you get that recording, "If you'd like to make a call, please hang up and dial…" Of course I'd like to make a call! That's why I'm ON THE PHONE!

It's also important to note that Fleming Textiles, an ancient Scottish lace-making company, was contracted to weave special ropes for dragging errant satellites out of orbit, and that these ropes are called "Terminator Tethers." This is important because I don't write another column that I could work it into.

Property lines tend to be straight, or follow roads. But microclimates don't care about man-made boundaries. Thanks to NASA, by looking at incredibly detailed, infrared satellite images, a grower can now pick out tiny pockets of difference. Participating wineries have confirmed that they really can taste marked differences when they divide vineyards along these new lines. Aerial studies confirm what vintners have observed for centuries: Periodic water-stress results in tastier grapes and the feebler the vine, the better the wine. The images are also proving helpful in spotting and treating infestations before they completely take over a vineyard.

Undoubtedly these tools will result in a better product for the consumer, and we have science to thank for that. So remember, when moss grows on the south side of the satellite, the bottle will see its shadow.

RESPECT THE GRAPES
It's their show

IF YOU LOVE WINE, but you're tired of sponging up spills and washing glasses, not to mention all that unpleasant swallowing, take heart. Thanks to new technology from the Bureau Interprofessionnel des Vins de Bourgogne (BIVB), virtual wine is on its way. Connect to their site and your special software will detect tags, causing your hand-held diffuser to release wine fragrances. It's still a little crude, they admit, but their Vineyard of Burgundy program will make you swear you're "right in the middle of a wood or a cellar or in a glass of white Burgundy."

People are always trying to outsmart grapes. Winemakers with egos and equipment labor at spinning inferior grapes into gold. More than one California winery uses *Reserve* not for their best fruit, but for some tarted-up, oaky forensic statement about the winemaker's fingerprints.

Science works wonders, but for delicious wine, give me a farmer. Since most wine we drink these days is young, we expect it to taste like fruit. And good fruit is still made in the vineyard. I recently visited two wineries, both alike in dignity, in fair Victoria, where we lay our scene. Victoria, Australia, to be specific, one of the cooler growing regions Down Under. The vineyards and olive groves of Montalto form a natural amphitheatre, sloping down to a spring-fed stream and wetlands teaming with protected woodland critters. They'll make you a picnic basket and send you strolling through the herb gardens and fruit and nut orchards that supply their restaurant. It's the sort of place where people propose. The showbiz would make me skittish about wine quality if it weren't the norm at so many Australian wineries.

Harvest has begun, but luckily there's still fruit on the vine. As a friend of mine says: "Never buy a vineyard in winter. It's like buying a woman in Pakistan."

Owner John Mitchell left the business world for viticulture seven years ago. He lifts a corner of the white netting that shields the remaining fruit from enophilic birds, and we duck into a row of Pinot Noir. He's changing the previous owner's trellis system to get more sun on the grapes. They hang in plump, purple bunches, evenly sized and ripened, covered with a soft white film. I pick a few to eat. They pop like caviar in my mouth, releasing their perfumy-sweet juice.

Mitchell has planted a bunch of Pinot clones, each with a strikingly different flavor. He's worried about some early-season sunburn, but he has to search up and down the rows to find me evidence: a few tiny, unformed grapes, hidden in a heavy cluster.

The tasting room is not grand or fussy. It has a counter, water and somewhere to spit, all I require. The Chardonnays explode with tropical, tangerine/lime exuberance that erases all memory of how boring this grape can be. The Pinot Noirs are sublime, all perfume and candied lollipops. How much oak, I ask him, what sort, how long? But he's as vague on this part as he was passionate and informed in the vineyard.

The second winery is right next door. The weather, the soil, even the vines planted are identical. This owner spends barely five minutes showing me down a row. I just have time to notice that the clusters are green, purple, blue and red. Some grapes are big, some small, and quite a few shriveled and torched by the sun. Unless someone handpicks each grape, all this goes into the wine, I think.

And, indeed, the wine I sample has little fruit to smell or taste, but coats my mouth with the rasping tannin of unripe grape seeds. A few are no more than a mouthful of toasted oak. Quite a contrast to the ripe fruit so lovingly tended next door. I wonder if it would taste better in front of my computer at home, enhanced by a few whiffs from the hand-held BIVB diffuser. Nah.

E PLURIBUS VINUM
Single vineyards versus blends

THE PROPAGANDA POURS IN DAILY: "For Immediate Release! CJ Westerfleece to oversee production of Loaded Gun Red, from the vineyard where founder Boots McCauley tripped on a clone and shot out his own left nostril. This elite, single-vineyard Syrah will be fermented in Bulgarian oak thimbles by thirty virgins, stared at by a goat for six months and stirred daily with ostrich feathers."

I know what you're thinking: Why, suddenly, the emphasis on single vineyards? Even as we celebrate diversity and coalesce rainbows, we seem to believe that exclusive is better. Prestige is reserved for the most specific appellations. "California" just doesn't have the same ring as "Echézeaux." Actually, it's not a bad rule of thumb, and God knows, in wine, we need all of those we can get. It's also a nice stroke of marketing.

Despite the breathless press releases, however, "single-vineyard" is not synonymous with quality. At worst, these wines can be downright weird. Or simply one-dimensional—trading away the complexity of a blend from different vineyards for label cachet. At best, they're distinctive. Raise your hand, though, if you can truly taste the difference between chalky soil and gravel without trying the wines side by side. Or even then.

It's not just vineyards that have gotten hoity-toity. Grape varieties, too, tend to hang with their kind in this country. A wine labeled "Cabernet Sauvignon" gets respect. But woe unto "Murray's Table Red," even if it's a classic Bordeaux blend.

Why are we hung up on single-grape wines? Marketing, again. After a few American decades of "chablis" and "burgundy" as authentic as krab and cheez, wineries decided it was time to come clean and just tell us what grapes were in the bottle—a practice known as varietal labeling. (Note: Grapes come in *varieties*. Only wine is *varietal*. If you confuse the two, you're liable to draw derisive laughs from the three people who actually care about this distinction.)

Europe, meanwhile, has always blended. Some of the world's most famous wines—the likes of Hermitage, Bordeaux and the Turbo-Tuscans—are mergers. Châteauneuf-du-Pape is a stew of up to thirteen varieties, including white grapes Bourboulenc and Marsanne as well as Syrah, Grenache, Mourvèdre, Dopey, Sneezy and Pluto.

Champagne, too, is all about fusion. Varieties, colors, vineyards and years team up to bring you a "house style." It's not unusual for a non-vintage brut to best its vintage cousin.

What's the advantage of blending? A good winemaker has both palate and palette. Whether aiming for a reliable, homogeneous mix, or collaborating with nature to create a unique masterpiece, she needs to bridge the gap between what grapes offer and what consumers want. Lack color? Kick up the Petit Verdot. Need aromatics? A dab of Cab Franc. The challenges change with the vintage.

If you're still determined to go it alone, you should know that a wine labeled, for instance, "Sauvignon Blanc" can have between 10 percent and 25 percent alien grapes aboard (varies by state). Even a single-vineyard, 100 percent Cabernet Sauvignon is a blend of sorts: new and old oak, perhaps; French and American, stainless and wood, ebony and ivory.

I wouldn't worry too much about whether your wine plays well with others. I mean, can't we all just hold hands and get along?

JUICY OR ELEGANT?
The hang-time debate

THERE'S A STRANGE BUSINESS dividing wine critics these days. Ostensibly a disagreement about "hang-time," or how long you should wait before picking grapes, the deeper issue is what wine is truly supposed to be: fruit drink, or sophisticated chemical transcendence?

During the historical epoch running from the first wheel to the first cork, roughly a squillion years, wine resembled either white Zinfandel or cooking sherry: sweet, fizzy, pink and guzzled down fast or oxidized and cooked to stabilization, in the sense that it couldn't get any worse. Its main purposes were to keep you from being killed by cholera or giardia in the water supply, and, as today, to take your mind off work. Good taste was a distant third and required additions of honey, pine tar, salt and you don't even want to think about what else.

The invention of bottles and corks ushered in a new era

of wine cellars. Given Europe's unpredictable climate, prudence often dictated an early harvest, before grapes were lost to mold, rain or hungry birds. The resulting wines, unripe, tannic and acidic, usually needed years of mellowing before they were drinkable, and by that time had lost any resemblance to fruit. This sort of wine, still the template of traditionalists, might smell like wet earth under a log, dry dust blowing through a corral, or bacon and animal sweat. It enters your mouth like water, but if you wait, the best ones unfold with the intricacy and grace of origami.

They're called "food wines," because liveliness and low alcohol make them refreshing, or in some cases, because it takes food to smother the battery acid oozing from their core.

Then, along came sunny Australia and America, followed by technological advances for picking riper fruit and correcting imbalance, and a new-style wine was born: thick as chocolate pudding with an explosion of fruit as cheeky and unexpected as an ambush-spritz from the perfume girl at Macy's. A standout in tastings, this wine garners big numbers and impressive reviews. It's known as a "sipping wine," because its high alcohol and intense flavors simply won't pipe down enough to blend in with the harmony of a meal.

Which style is correct? Ask a producer and the answer is invariably "ours." If their fruit gets ripe, they assure you wine is all about freshness and concentration. If it doesn't particularly, then elegance is the buzzword and if you find their wine dull you simply lack refinement.

What's got critics choosing sides right now is a trend in California to leave grapes hanging on the vine longer than ever before. As grape skins thicken, they develop more flavor, color and extraction, as well as sugar, which translates to higher alcohol. The result is a lush, intense, over-the-top drink. But is it wine?

The bigger-to-better correlation in the rest of life is in constant flux. Voluminous record collections and ceiling-high woofers and tweeters, emblems of the swinging bachelor of yore, now tuck neatly inside a four-inch iPod. Cell phones, too, started big and went tiny. Yet now, early adapters corral camera, organizer and email into the bloated form of a late-harvest BlackBerry.

Pity poor critics, who must decide what's correct and officially in good taste. Raters of art, music and food alike tend to laud what's most difficult to produce and understand, always a fastidious step or two ahead of public taste.

You, though, are free to follow your yens and curiosities. When I do seminars, I get just as big a kick tuning Americans in to the seductive whisper of old and subtle wine as I do giving Europeans permission to just go ahead and enjoy the fruit. Proclaiming one style better seems as silly as asking, "What should music be: Mozart or that danged rock and roll?" Answer: all of that and more.

RIGHT TO THE SOURCE
Be treated like a vineyard VIP

IF YOU HAVEN'T YET HAD THE PLEASURE, it's time to visit wine country. Yours. Your local region is no doubt a place of beauty and charm (sometimes transcending the charm of the actual wine, considering all fifty states have wineries). Too many tourists take to the tasting trail with no plan, and wind up exhausted and overwhelmed. Follow these steps, instead, to get the most out of the experience, as well as VIP treatment.

In wine country, gargantuan factories often sit cheek by jowl with ramshackle one-man affairs. Your route should take in both, and leave time for lunch.

Cardinal rule: Thou Shalt Spit. Practice in the shower. Swallowers end up dazed and fried, too marinated to think. Wineries like this. They want you to get happy and buy a lot of wine, so sometimes you have to ask for the spittoon.

Take notes, or all those "unforgettable" wines will be a blur the next day. Besides, the very act of scribbling strikes fear and awe into the hearts of producers. They are desperately hoping for a write-up, even in *Practical Welding*.

If there's a tour, skip it. You did that stuff in fourth grade at the Natural History Museum. That doesn't mean you don't want to see the winery. You just need the right host. Check out who's pouring. The "cellar rat," a young factotum, prostrating himself for love of the business, can be good. Get him off his rote speech by asking if his job is hard, and what he likes about it. Be sympathetic; you might root out some dirt. Beware, though, anyone in marketing. All you'll get is a volley of pre-programmed clichés.

What you really want is the owner or, better, the winemaker. Engage this person. Your level of wine expertise is irrelevant—curiosity is what counts. Some openers: "What's different about your winery? Does being a Superfund Clean-up Site affect the size of your grapes?"

No doubt the label has a story, but they've told it a thousand times, and it's probably bogus. Ask, instead, to see the vineyards. Winemakers are happiest there, in their natural habitat. Ask if you can try a grape off the vine. Find out about the trellis system and irrigation. If you're on a mountain, they would love to tell you how hard it is to farm and why it's worth it. If you're in a valley, skip the question—they'll go on the defensive saying, "Valleys *are too* as good as mountains!"

There will be a local issue concerning road access, endangered species or erosion control. They will have a passionate opinion. Listen to it. You can then riff on this theme at the next winery you visit: "Had any run-ins, lately, with the fungus-rights movement?"

The vineyard is foreplay for the tasting room. A tourist will march right in and demand, say, red. You, on the other hand, VIP, will say, "What do you think I should taste?" The answer may be way outside your normal scope. Flow with it. It probably resonates beautifully with the local terroir.

You need not praise the wine as you taste. This is a good time to take intense, cryptic notes, in Morse code if anyone is peeking. If you talk, phrase your observations carefully: For instance, "Tell me about the exuberant acid in the Pinot Grigio!" rather than, "Oh my God, my fillings are melting!"

By now, the love you've inspired in the winemaker should have swollen up to the point where he's compelled to offer you an exclusive tasting: the last bottle of 1974 Concord, perhaps, or his six-year-old daughter's first single-vintage bottling. He might confess that his real passion is Madeira, and shyly pour you his version. You must pronounce it extraordinary.

If you're taken to the cellar for barrel samples, consider this a great honor. Don't expect barrel wine to taste good. It might be hazy, still fermenting, or simply tasteless. The key questions here are, "How do you expect this to change and develop?" and "How does it compare to last year?"

Upon leaving, it's good manners to buy a bottle or two, and to courier a few of their brochures, pricelists and business cards to an off-site dumpster. As you drive away, warm in the glow of the royal treatment, perhaps clutching a gift—a bottle pressed into your hands at the last minute—you'll realize that you've learned a heap, discovered some new wines, and maybe even made a friend for life.

TWO TRACKS
Are factories crushing the artisan? And de-stemming him?

I'VE HAD IT UP TO HERE with complaints about faceless, corporate wines. It's about time someone stood up for them.

A bland tide they may be, yet they've raised all boats. Old World artisans, for all their "I am but a shepherd; the wine makes itself" talk, in reality follow recipes created by millennia of trial and error. New World wineries must tackle questions about varieties, yeasts, timing, bugs and bacteria. The investment of giants in clean-up, clone testing and other science helps the little guy enormously.

While the wines that convulse us in religious ecstasy tend to come from small, quirky producers, we forget how much independent wine is perfectly dreadful. "Tasting of place" is not always a good thing; *terroir*, after all, is French for "*Merde* happens."

In search of that sublime experience, however, we are willing to risk all. Like rats forever stomping the lever that intermittently dispenses cocaine, we keep opening bottles, hoping for another glimpse of God. Or at least something drinkable. Those of us in the business do more harm to our wrists pulling corks than we do to our pocketbooks. We scrutinize vintage charts and study harvest conditions in Cahors. We are, according to a marketing guy in Australia, High Interest Drinkers.

But we are preaching to a world of Low Interest Drinkers. We tell them wine should be quirky, esoteric, individual. We encourage them to branch out, be adventurous. "Forget ratings!" we say, "Just drink what you like!" Then we shove them into a store where the California Chardonnay aisle alone runs twenty furlongs before you round the turn to Tasmanian white, Douro red, Uzbekistan sparkling...

The great swath of America between the foodie coasts sees wine as snotty and intimidating. They're terrified they'll be branded Cork Dork of the Year if they don't order right, but they're damned if they can keep up with what right is. First pink was bad; now it's good. The dank sweat of Football Locker Room is dreadful, but the belching diesel of Greyhound Bus Terminal is heavenly. Furthermore, on a moral scale they place wine somewhere between naughty and evil. Hardly an everyday, healthy part of the meal.

History is partly to blame. Early American growing efforts were foiled by the root louse phylloxera. Wine became the province of those wealthy enough to import from Europe, while the masses made do with beer and cider. What wine we did manage—proto-Manischewitz concoctions of Scuppernong, Concord and sugar—couldn't hope to survive months on the rutted wagon trails that led west.

Whiskey could. Raw on the throat and packing alcohol like a sheriff packs iron, whiskey was not what you'd call a refreshing, digestive, food beverage. On the contrary, it was banned from the dinner table—banished to card-playing, fist-fighting dens of iniquity where the idea was to slug back as much as you could before falling down or throwing up. Pretty much exactly where beer stands today in our establishments of higher learning.

There was a glimmer of hope for wine culture, when late-19th-century immigrants reached California and planted their Zinfandel vine atop her, but that was quickly quashed by Prohibition. A generation of drinkers and their quaffing songs was lost and acres of vines uprooted. Come Repeal, beer could sprint off in a matter of days while wine needed four years in the vineyard just to tie her shoelaces.

Few Americans learned wine the European way, at grandpa's knee. Most of our closets hide an embarrassing set of training-wheels: from Bartles & J to Lancer's Rosé to white Zin, which seemed so sophisticated.

We want more Americans to drink wine. It is from among the clueless masses with their gluey glasses that the wine gods pluck their next candidate for connoisseurship. Do you sip your Coke, thinking, "It's got the typical minerality and bubble structure of the Michigan plant, but I prefer the simplicity of the Ohio."? Of course not; it's all the same. For wine to weave itself, Coke-like, into the daily fabric of life, it must be three things: cheap, unintimidating and reliable.

That does not describe the output of the quirky artiste, but rather the great spewing rivers made possible by the economy of scale of the Australian mega-conglomerates. The majority won't bother to learn about tannins and petrol and malolactic conversion. They just want something they can afford and pronounce, like Yellowtail or Two-Buck Chuck.

Haven't you ever been homesick in a foreign country? You've had your fill of deliciously exotic ethnic cuisine and picturesque customs and for just one moment you'd give your right arm to spot the familiar logo of Walgreen's, where you could march right in and buy jock-itch powder, tampons or denture cream without having to explain your symptoms, with the aid of phrasebook and growing crowd of helpful natives, to the quaint aspirin grinder in the alley. Stop picking on Walgreen's wine. It can thrive right alongside Priorat and Alsace—we'll all be richer for it. Let a thousand corks pop!

Part 2
Red & White Grapes

THIS SECTION IS ABOUT TABLE WINES, the reasonably dry ones you drink with a meal, which usually involves a table. Or, in my case, a keyboard, as cracker crumbs stuck under my Shift key can attest. What's with the weird selection? How come no Chardonnay or Merlot? Because I didn't feel like writing about them, OK?

CENTURY CLUB
Hey! Look at me! I'm a grape, too, you know.

RED, WHITE, PINK…it's been like that forever. I don't know about you, but I'm ready for wine in designer colors. Mauve. Puce. How about striped wine? Though they had neither stripes nor polka dots, the wines at a recent blind tasting contest I won were every bit as strange.

To accomplish the feat, I mustered all my training and experience, taking copious notes on color, smell, taste, mouth-feel and finish, and tapping into my knowledge of terroir and climate in the world's wine regions. None of which helped in the least. Multiple choice answers made it clear the wines all came from grapes I'd never heard of.

The competition took place at the inaugural dinner of the Wine Century Club. New members were initiated to much ceremony and awarded engraved diplomas and silver tastevins on neck-ribbons. To qualify, you had to have tasted at least a hundred different grapes. An impressive feat, if not quite as daunting as the requirements for extreme organizations like the Polar Bears (nope, forget it) or the Mile High Club (yup, remember it).

The Century Club is the brainchild of Steve and Deborah DeLong, whose mission is to turn you on to new grapes. Their first effort was the Wine Grape Varietal Table, a charming marriage of art and geekery that organizes 180 grapes by weight, acidity, color, tannins and country. It began as a series of Post-It notes on the wall, constantly shifting as experts and idiots weighed in with their opinions. It's now a handsome, frame-worthy chart that all wine lovers should own.

The movie *Sideways* may have halted the Merlot reflex plaguing our country for lo these many years, but it merely turned the herd and sent it stampeding off after Pinot Noir. While that path is being beaten to a pulp, alternate routes bloom with gorgeous grapes you've never heard of.

Just as the acne-faced nerd leaves the toxic environment of high school prom and finds studliness in the world of IT, so certain grapes—Malbec and Grenache for example—turn from the thankless role of blending grape at home to stardom in other soils. Others, even more obscure, are doing what they've always done, only better. Each of the following grapes deserves its own column, but a short intro will have to do for now.

Among whites: crisp, spanking Silvaner and Scheurebe from Germany; Languedoc's "lip-stinging" Picpoul—the perfect picnic pour; Torrontés—Argentina's fragrant, flowery alternative to Chardonnay; and dozens from Italy, including Campania's nutty Fiano and flinty Greco di Tufo, the herbal, apple-y Erbaluce of Caluso and a trio of Vibrant Vs—Vernaccia, Verdicchio and Vermentino.

Reds you should shake hands with include the ancient,

dark, peppery Pineau d'Aunis of the Loire; berry-fragrant Bonarda from Argentina: the plummy tobacco and leather of Lagrein from Trentino-Alto Adige; Umbria's cherry-spicy Sagrentino; and Sicily's answer to Syrah, the inky-violet Nero d'Avola.

Don't let the strange names spook you; no one else can pronounce them either. One up-and-comer, Hungary's Cserszegi Fuszeres, is even bottled as The Unpronounceable Grape.

Become an eno-explorer and before you know it, you, too, could be eligible for the Century Club. You're probably closer than you think, since so many wines are blends. Bordeaux and Port, for instance, commonly use five different grapes and Châteauneuf-du-Pape contains up to thirteen.

So how did I manage to win? Ancient, SAT-honed strategies saved me in the end: when in doubt, choose #3 or a word that starts with "S." That and pondering aloud while scrutinizing judges for that inadvertent flinch known to poker players as the "tell."

I'll leave you with a pro's tip for your next blind tasting: If it comes to a tie, fold your entry in accordion pleats. When they draw the winner out of a hat, the pointy parts on your ballot will stick up and make it more likely to be chosen. It worked for me.

CALL OF THE WILD & CRAZY
Aromatic, musky whites

YOU GOTTA LOVE the optimistic spirit of the little eBay ad that pops up on your Google screen helpfully offering, for instance: Great Deals on New and Used **MUSK OX**! My search for this animal was an unplanned detour in a story about Muscadelle, Muscadet, Muscat and other musk-ular sounding wines.

The smell of Muscat is often described as "musky," but I

wasn't buying it. After all, isn't musk all about sweaty armpits and animal pheromones? What does it have to do with the flowery, perfumy, *grapey* aroma of Muscat? The term "foxy" often describes indigenous American grapes because of their Latin name, *vulpine*. This has led more than one writer to find notes of wet fur—even slyness—in the wines.

Vitis vinifera is the European species that Cabernet, Chardonnay, Merlot, Riesling and virtually all the great, and even some indifferent wine grapes belong to. The USA, on the other hand, is home to eating grapes, such as *V. labrusca* and *V. vulpes*, which you may know as Concord, Catawba and the like.

But while that wine is sweet and refreshing and often pleasant, it's not even in *vinifera*'s zip code. You can vinify cherries, peaches and kumquats (if you can figure out what they are) but you won't come close to the complexity of *vinifera*.

We can detect over 10,000 different components in *vinifera* wines, which is a lucky break for wine critics who would get pretty bored writing, "tastes like wine," over and over again. Many of these chemicals have lock-and-key connections in our brain which work something like this: imagine the smell of Sunkist as a key that fits into a lock in your brain, causing you to think, "Orange!" Now, *vinifera* takes a counterfeit key and sticks it in the same slot, causing you to say, "Hints of pungent orange peel tiptoe bracingly across the midpalate," while your brain thinks, "Orange!" It also has the key to sauerkraut, filter pad and diesel, according to the official Wine Aroma Wheel. Incidentally, the Wheel makes mention of skunk, but no word on foxes.

I smelled a muskrat. But to be certain, I thought I'd better make sure I knew what musk smelled like. Out of the question was a whiff of the real thing, harvested, incidentally, not from the musk ox—who secretes a "musky odor" from a gland under his eyes when he's excited—but from the tiny, endangered musk deer who secretes odor from a gland near his testicles, presumably not when he's bored. It's not only rare and exorbitantly expensive, but, like elephant ivory, it's illegal. Perfumes today all use synthetic versions.

So does just about every scented household product. This is not so you'll go into rut at the sight of a dust-mop. It's because musk is uncannily good at carrying other aromas. Drip some in a jar that's been empty for months and the original contents come wafting back. A drop in the toilet could cause even iron janitors to blanch.

To learn its smell, I take a field trip to the mall. The number of stores devoted to Ayurvedic lotions and Dead Sea bath salts, to natural sponges and lavender foot pumice is staggering. Do people really spend this much time in the bath? Or are these products like so much fruitcake: forever gifted, never used?

"Essential oils" sound so pure, as though they were squeezed right out of the ginger root or teaberry branch they represent. Actually, they're complex blends of chemicals. I sniff vials labeled "White Musk" and "Japanese Musk." They smell vaguely sweet, a little soapy. Nothing remotely husky in their tone.

"I want to smell musk," I tell a salesgirl. She scopes out the store and comes back to report that nothing they carry really smells musky to her. When I ask what musk smells like she answers, "It smells like, well, *musky.*" The same tautology is proffered in store after store; along with the admittance that not only is their musk not the real thing, it doesn't even smell like the real fake.

Some who came of age in the '70s feel passionately about musk, confessing an atavistic longing for the hairy chest oozing animal attraction from under an armor of gold medallions. And so it is that I quit pussyfooting and go right to the source: the perfume aisle at Rite Aid, where Jovan and Coty, king and queen of drugstore musk, promise to turn women into foxes and men into studs in Stetsons.

And these, too, are just vaguely sweet. Nothing I know of

dusky, sweaty passion is in these bottles. Either they're lying, or I'm among the estimated ten to forty percent of the population *anosmic* to musk: i.e., I can't smell it.

Walking home from the mall I cross a tiny chunk of country—thigh-high grass and trees, wedged between two developments. Out of a clump of weeds bounds a fox. He pours across the lot, a red flame with a puff of smoky white tail floating behind him. The smell is unmistakable. You would give your dog a bath if he rolled in it. It is musk. And Muscat grapes smell nothing like it.

Ancient pundit Pliny, the go-to guy when you need a Latin quote, dubbed Muscat "the grape of bees," because they were drawn to its sweetness. So, presumably, were flies—*musca* in Latin. One etymological theory has the grape named for the flies swarming around it. Which would certainly make all those "musky" tasting notes a little silly.

I'm looking forward to the day you can Google a scent and actually smell it. It would sure be simpler than a field trip to determine the difference between the bouquet of Musk Ox: Bored, and Musk Ox: Excited.

Part II—The Grapes

Muscat, Muscadet, Muscadelle. All for one and one for all? Hardly. These are separate terms that encompass an enormous variety of red, white, sweet, dry and fizzy wines. Add in aliases like Muscatel, Moscato and Muskateller, and sorting out who's who becomes quite a puzzle.

Let's start by reformatting our cerebral hard drive: In a cliché file deep in our brains, "Muscat," "Muscatel" and "cheap" share a folder. Delete it. While you're in there, why not toss out "Champale," as well.

Ready? We'll start with Muscat, a name that comprises a huge family of grapes, perhaps the oldest cultivated ones we know, with origins shrouded in the ancient mists of Persia and

Omar Khayyam. Its members are black, red, white and even table grapes. Some of its more familiar names are Muscat of Alexandria, Muscat de Frontignan and Orange Muscat.

It's the only variety to make wine that smells like its grapes. Chardonnay grapes smell nothing like Chardonnay wine, nor do Merlot grapes resemble the final product. But sniff a glass of Muscat, and you could be standing right in the vineyard.

Muscat, like Gewürztraminer, is classified as *aromatic*. It makes a fabulous starter grape for aspiring blind-tasters because its perfumy aroma is unique and easy to recognize. Good thing, as it shows up in the damnedest places:

Dry: Alsace makes bone-dry Muscat with rich body and a fragrant, flowery nose. Très exotique.

Fizzy: Italy's Moscato d'Asti is a classier cousin of Asti Spumante, with smaller bubbles and less sugar. A similar, lightly sweet bubbly is Clairette de Die from the Rhône valley. Both have about half the alcohol of the average California table wine, which makes them great thirst-quenchers on a hot day and useful for lunch.

Sweet: Late harvest dessert Muscats show up in Alsace, in Germany as Muskateller, and in California, whence the Muscatel that no train-hopping hobo would be without. Ignore it. The good stuff bears the name of the variety: Orange, White or Black Muscat, for instance, or just a proprietary name, like Eos's *Tears of Dew*.

Fortified: In Spain, Muscat is one of only three grapes allowed in sherry, but you can't really taste it there. South Africa produces the Muscat-based Constantia, the most sought-after dessert wine in Europe during the days of Napoleon and Dickens and now reputedly Nelson Mandela's favorite. From France comes Muscat de Beaumes de Venise, a lighter dessert wine from Provence, usually delightful for the price.

Liquor: Peru and Chile both claim Pisco, a Muscat-based, distilled spirit, as their own. Mexico's version is Metaxa.

On to our second Muscateer: Muscadelle, also a rosy-nose, aromatic grape, but curiously enough, unrelated to Muscat. It shows up in two places:

Dry & sweet: In Bordeaux, Muscadelle is blended with Sauvignon Blanc and Semillon to make dry, white wines such as Graves, as well as the mega-rich dessert wines of Sauternes.

Fortified: Australia has been making a thick, molasses-brown, fortified dessert wine from Muscadelle since 1820, called—just to muddle things up even more—Tokay. Tokaj happens to be the name of a famous Hungarian dessert wine, and Tokay Pinot Gris is what they call Pinot Grigio in Alsace. Then there's Italy's Tocai Friulano. Try not to think about it too much.

Our third Muscateer is easier: Muscadet, which sounds similar, but isn't at all. It's the name of a wine, not a grape. The grape is Melon de Bourgogne and the wine is crisp, dry and even a little salty, with none of the Muscat aromatics. It's found only in the Loire valley and ranges from mediocre and dull to beautifully refreshing, especially in the Sèvre et Maine appellation. It's famous for its affinity to oysters.

You may not remember all the branches we've discussed, but one sniff should at least tell you if you're climbing the right family tree. Watch out for foxes.

CREAM & PUNISHMENT
Sauvignon Blanc hurts so good

MY FRIEND BOB describes Catholic confession as the place where you go to tell a complete stranger everything you spend most of your energy lying about to everyone else. I'm envious of this opportunity for a drive-through soul wash. My only tool for exorcising guilt is…actually being good. This lasts about five minutes and then there I go, performing an illegal function again. Turning my column in late, for example.

What I would give for such a magic tollbooth! I imagine gathering up the spare sins lying around the floor of my life, tossing them in a basket and driving out the other side thinking only of the road ahead! Four out of five Freudians agree: what I need is a good spanking. It's the only way to explain why all winter long, while other wine drinkers cozy up to comforting Port and claret, I drink icy-cold Sauvignon Blanc.

Sauvignon Blanc spanks. It's the gin and tonic of wines, replacing G&T's squeeze of fresh lime with a stiff swat of acid. It's perfect after tennis in the hot sun. Sometimes it even spangles with a hint of CO_2 left over from fermentation, or (cover your ears, you don't want to know), added later for that effect. No matter. It works. The sting makes you want to slap your cheeks and go "Ah!" like guys in aftershave commercials.

Hidden for years within the inscrutable French appellation system, Sauvignon Blanc is the main ingredient in Graves, Sancerre and Pouilly-Fumé. These are lovely, elegant wines, but the grape remains fairly neutral—mostly cold, hard steel, with the occasional whiff of ocean brine in the Loire and some mellowing Semillon in Bordeaux.

But go south of the equator and all hell breaks loose. Nowhere does SB snap, crackle and pop like in New Zealand. The smell is often described as cat pee on a gooseberry bush. The cat part is true, though strangely pleasant. But since most Americans have never met a gooseberry outside of jam and English fairy tales, a different descriptor is in order. Certainly citrus: lemon, lime and especially grapefruit. "Zing" feels right. Or try this optical illusion: If you juxtapose two colors of equal saturation from opposite sides of the color wheel, just the right red and blue for example, the line where they meet appears to vibrate. That's New Zealand Sauvignon Blanc.

Kiwis, like their Australian neighbors, don't give a fig about tradition. They're bravely leading the push to screwcaps. So don't be surprised to find some of their very best SB in twist-offs.

It must be something in the hemisphere, because the grape also dances with the same verve plus a tropical, tangerine shimmy in South Africa and South America. Especially Chile's Casablanca Valley. Watch those Chileans, though, or they'll tart the thing up with sugar and oak for what they call, with equal parts hope and scorn, "The American Taste."

As for America, Sauvignon Blanc arrived here at a time when the theory was, "If it doesn't move, barrel it." If you smother lemon gelato with enough hot butterscotch sauce, it'll taste generically vanilla; and so it is that some American SBs are dead ringers for Chardonnay.

So, it comes in many styles, not all of which pack the same bitch-slap; it's not hard to grow, and there's lots of it around. So why did it lie down and let Pinot Grigio overtake Chardonnay as America's best-selling white?

Robert Mondavi locked onto the main problem that keeps it off best-seller lists in America: we're afraid to pronounce it. I know that sounds stupid. Yet ease of ordering was a vital part of the enormous popularity of Merlot in America.

Mondavi changed "Sauvignon" to the far less intimidating "Fumé," and sales took off. That was 1967. Since he didn't trademark the name, lots of wineries use it now. Fumé means smoke, and the fumes in this case come from toasted barrels. So you can expect Fumé Blanc to be a low-acid, creamy custard, which I think defeats the whole purpose, but there I go getting uppity again.

Whichever style you prefer, you'll get twice the white at half the price. You may even find absolution. And who among us couldn't use a good spanking?

SECOND COMING
The two lives of Malbec

AT THE AGE OF TWELVE, I did something all embarrassed preteens dream about and few outside the witness protection program ever get a chance at: I reinvented myself. Fed up with my shoddy grades, my mother uprooted me from my uniformed girls' academy—the kind of place where your status was a coefficient of dodge-ball throwing velocity and midterm math grades—and sent me off to a sort of new-wave experiment in learning where you went around in bare feet and called your teacher Bob. Unless, of course, his name was Sally.

It was the best thing that ever happened to me. Along with the enchanting and terrifying presence of boys, came the beauty of starting with a clean slate. No longer was I the loner who slept through math and found diagramming sentences a complete waste of time. Transplanted, I became a popular, vivacious biology whiz, admired by all for my ability to map out a phrase in Latin or English. I had found my people.

All of you who long to pull into the pit stop of life and have your reputation rotated: your vinous patron saint is Malbec.

Malbec is a grape with a second-rate role in Europe. In Bordeaux it's a blender, little more than Viagra for flaccid reds. Its main home is further south, the region of *Cahors*. (Keep the S silent and pronounce the H like you're receiving the Heimlich maneuver.)

In medieval times, Malbec was cooked into a syrupy-concentrate they called Black Wine. For a brief burst of 1850s glory, Cahors counted 140,000 acres of Malbec and was getting almost as important as Bordeaux. But then came the root-louse *phylloxera*, munching its way through Europe like Pac-Man, and when the dust settled, Bordeaux had its act together while Cahors was still reeling.

Further demoralized by freak frosts in 1956 that killed

another mass of vines, Cahors nevertheless became an official AOC appellation in 1971, one that requires 70 percent Malbec grapes, with Merlot and Tannat making up the balance.

Except at tip-top levels, Cahors isn't very good. Thin-skinned and sensitive, Malbec longs for heat and sun, and craves well-irrigated, well-drained soil. Without these conditions, it's extremely susceptible to frost damage, downy mildew, bunch rot and other nuisances. You'd be cranky, too.

Meanwhile, in a parallel universe, Malbec cuttings had been smuggled to Argentina in 1868. The pure air and high altitude of Mendoza lets in intense sunlight. Hot days, cool nights and long growing seasons build complexity.

Malbec took one look and knew it was home. Because here's the thing: Cabernet, Merlot and the rest of *that* gang all come from a common ancestor. Malbec is genetically different. It has a Latin soul. With a little encouragement it will lie on the beach with its shirt off, whisper poetry in your ear, kiss with passion and tango till dawn.

In Argentina, thanks to both mutation and climate differences, Malbec is rich and complex, with luxuriously smooth tannins and ripeness Europe can only dream about. Vivid plum and raspberry aromas give way to a darker edge of licorice, coffee, chocolate and leather. Joyful to drink now, it also ages gracefully for decades.

Then there's the price. An acre of Argentine vineyard costs a fraction of its French and California counterparts. Labor there is cheap and plentiful. So while a decent Cahors can set you back $70, the same amount buys you ten terrific bottles from Mendoza, where even the cheap stuff is good.

France has noticed. A top Cahors producer just successfully lobbied to allow the word "Malbec" on his labels, giving a former nobody grape star billing over an appellation that even the French don't much understand.

Why, given all the grapes available, do the French continue to torture Malbec? It seems to come down to that Frenchest of reasons: "But…we have always done it this way!" In contrast to the dashing Latin lover in Argentina, the top Malbec in Cahors marches along with austere, tannic purpose, humming mineral notes of iron, hot stones and tar, doing its buttoned-down best to be like Bordeaux. Most of it goes to Canada, Germany, Britain and Japan, who probably never *had* a Latin lover, anyway.

If you haven't either, it's time you spent the evening with an Argentine Malbec. And for some real fun while you sip, there's nothing quite like diagramming a sentence.

WHAT ZIN A NAME?
America's grape. Kind of. Not really.

WHOLE BOOKS HAVE BEEN WRITTEN about the mysterious origins of the Zinfandel grape, the only varietal considered unique to America. What about Concord grapes and whatever it was Leif Ericsson found in "Vinland?" Surely those were native Americans? Yes, but those are eating-grapes, belonging mostly to the species *labrusca*, noted for its Welch's-grapey aroma. The grapes that go into *real wines* (as distinguished from cherry or Manischewitz) are all of the species *vinifera*. Including Zinfandel. And they all originated in the Old World.

From people to plants to animals, how things got where they are today is a vast puzzle comprising shifting tectonic plates, mass extinctions, evolution, migration and other variables. Horses, for instance, evolved in America, crossed the Siberian land bridge into Eurasia and subsequently disappeared from the Americas entirely. They didn't come back until the Spaniards brought them over in ships in the 1400s where they were embraced by Native Americans, and are now considered a quintessential American icon, indispensable to both cowboys and Indians.

The idea of such a European-style grape as Zinfandel originating in America struck scientists as suspicious. Zinfandel appears in American writing as early as 1820. By the time the first wine boom swept California in the 1880s, no grape was more widely planted in America. Valiantly resisting both pestilence (their hardy rootstocks withstood an early *phylloxera* plague) and Prohibition (Zin was popular with home-winemakers, the only ones allowed to continue production); some Zin vines are among the oldest living grape producers in the world, making it possible to literally drink the Zins of our fathers.

Let's talk for a moment about white Zin. It's made from the pale insides of the grape with no red-skin contact. It may seem a travesty, and certainly did corrupt the Z word, it has proved a boon: It spared the life of those centenarian vines, which might have been ripped up and replanted to a trendier red. Sophisticated drinkers are back to drinking their Zin red, once again making it the most ubiquitous grape in America.

But...American? In 1967, a Californian enologist, strolling through a vineyard in Italy, thought the Primitivo grapes looked awfully familiar. A few scientific studies later, it was confirmed that Italian Primitivo and American Zinfandel were genetically identical. But they don't make identical wine. Quite a few differences have developed over the years. Recent research has pointed to a probable Croatian ancestor to both grapes. What probably happened was that some Balkan peasant brought cuttings to Austria, whence they migrated to Italy, to become Primitivo, and to America. Hence the Germanic name, *Zinfandel*. (Well you didn't think it was Iroquois, did you?) If you truly want American heritage you'll have to stick with corn, tomatoes and chocolate, all native to the New World.

But wherever the grape came from, the wine is truly our own. Bordeaux is the benchmark that Cabernet crafters strive for, and Riesling looks over its shoulder to Alsace and Germany. Port should taste like Portugal, and Champagne, well…duh. But Zinfandel has no Old World precedent, so Americans feel free to do whatever they want with it. Consequently, it's been made in every style conceivable. It can be a spicy, highly-alcoholic table red. It makes an excellent late harvest dessert wine. There's the infamous fizzy, pink white Zinfandel, and even a clear Grappa.

Because the grape clusters ripen unevenly, consistency has been a problem. Until recently, an unknown bottle could offer up anything from grassy, unripe flavors to an inky, raisinated brew, and its reputation suffered accordingly. But Zinophobic: take heart. Winemakers are taming this talented grape and offering complex single-vineyard wines as well as sophisticated blends. If you're not already an enthusiast, this is a great time to explore red Zinfandel. And be proud you're drinking something as American as apple…strudel.

QUÉ SYRAH, SHIRAZ
Which is which, like it matters

A FEW YEARS BACK everyone had Syrah pegged to be the next big trend. The Millennium Wine, they were calling it, a red to finally end the insipid reign of Merlot. After all, it's easy to drink, blissfully free of macho tannins and neither boring—like wines that come in only one style—nor annoying, like some quirky wines you have to be in the right mood for. So friendly it practically smiles back up at you, Syrah enjoys the sort of universal approval normally reserved for puppies and firemen. Compared to buttoned-down Cabernet and prima donna Pinot Noir, Syrah is a mensch.

What's more, it's easy to pronounce, which has a lot to do with the popularity of Merlot and Chardonnay. Yet, here it is, 2006, and I've yet to hear someone order "a Syrah" in generic lieu of "a red wine." What happened?

Sideways, for one thing; the buddy-flick that introduced the world to the beauty of the spit bucket. Thanks to Miles, the insufferable protagonist, Merlot has become the drink of social outcasts, while Pinot Noir is now the fashionable thing to do. Alas, Miles neglects to point out how elusive good Pinot Noir can be. So now normal people, who should have been swigging down friendly bottles of Syrah, are going around haggard and haunted about the eyes, trapped, like connoisseurs before them, in a lifetime quest for the wily and capricious Pinot Noir.

Another culprit is the name tangle: Syrah is not the same as *Petite Sirah*. DNA wine sleuths have dubbed Petite an imposter, really a distantly related grape called *Durif*. Syrah is, however, the same as *Shiraz*. This alternate name might come from the ancient Persian city of Shiraz, or from when cuttings arrived in Australia mistakenly labeled "Scyras." Anyway, that's what they call it in Australia, although they say Shee-raaz and we say Shur-oz and let's call the whole thing off.

Eeether or ayther way, the grape is ubiquitous because, for one thing, producers love it. An easy keeper, it's so vigorous they periodically have to wrestle it to the ground so it doesn't turn into a jungle when it should be putting its energy into fruit. It's happy in all temperatures. There's no benchmark style, like Bordeaux for Cab and Burgundy for Chardonnay, so winemakers feel free to experiment.

Warm climates bring out a fruit cocktail of plum, blueberry and blackberry, edged with peppery spice. Cooler regions produce chocolate, minerals, earth, smoked meat and licorice tones. Syrah hits the ground ready to drink, no mellowing or aging required. The price is terrific; exceptional Syrahs go for $20-$30, and pretty damn good ones for under $12. And there it is, on almost every wine list.

California went from 344 acres of the grape in 1990 to

over 14,000 today. It represents 40 percent of all red growing in Australia, showing up there in everything from $2 boxes to the fabulously expensive Penfolds Grange-Hermitage. That is, at least until France made them drop the "Hermitage" part, on the grounds that they had first dibs on the word. You see, French Syrah is concentrated in the Rhône Valley, in appellations like St. Joseph, Côte Rôtie and Crozes-Hermitage. Legend has it a 13th century French knight swiped Syrah cuttings while crusading in the holy land, probably somewhere near Persia. When he got home, planted, vinted and got a taste, he decided to make wine, not war, and spent the rest of his life holed up in his "hermitage," stirring lees.

You, on the other hand, have a life. If you don't want to devote hours of it to memorizing wine factoids, stop! Just order Syrah, the wine that nobody doesn't like. (If you write now and tell me you don't like it, you're probably the kind of person who kicks puppies. My fireman's going to come beat you up.)

KING CAB
Who died and made Cabernet king?

WHO DIED and made Cabernet king? Considered the noblest grape of all, Cabernet Sauvignon gets a higher price tag and more respect than anything else in the winery. It's poured last in tastings, and you're meant to ooh and aah, as though the winemaker had produced his kid's law school diploma. It's so well enthroned on top of the heap that we almost forget to ask why.

Reviewers, loath to give Zinfandel 93 points, award 100s to Cabernets as though its zenith were somehow more perfectly vinous than any heights some frivolous grape with a wacked-out Z-name could ever reach.

Cab inherits sheen from its key role in Bordeaux, where a yearly futures market infuses it with the gravitas of a Wall

Street commodity. Stratospheric auction prices reinforce its rep as a blue chip wine you can trust.

Unlike burly Barolo, the sort of wine that would take out the garbage and pull your car out of a ditch, Cabernet would hire someone. Focus groups link the grape with words like "important," "prized" and "serious." They'd pair the square-shouldered, buttoned-down bottle with steak, never silly food like sloppy Joes or bouillabaisse. But certain as consumers are about Cab's personality, they're shaky when you ask them what it tastes like.

Cabernet Sauvignon, offspring of a spontaneous mating of Cabernet Franc and Sauvignon Blanc, drifted from Central Asia into France around 1600, gaining its foothold in Bordeaux in the late 1700s with the appearance of the first great wine estates.

A century later, pioneers brought cuttings to California which had spread, by 1996, to over 40,000 acres. Moving in on quirky local grapes worldwide, Cab is spreading the gospel of International Style from South America to Australia to Eastern Europe. Goosing Garnacha in Spain, plumping Pinotage in South Africa and supering-up Tuscans in Italy, it now covers more than 400,000 acres around the globe.

Besides being a status- and quality-enhancer, Cabernet is also an easy keeper. It doesn't bloom until after spring frost and its loose clusters can be left hanging while tighter-bunched grapes are rescued from fall rain and rot. Appealing for growers. But what's so royal for drinkers?

Cab's small berries are light on juice and heavy on skin, where most of the flavor and color resides. The best Cabernets offer a bazaar of complex flavors ranging from black cherry, chocolate and cassis to cedar, green olives, pencil lead and tobacco. Oak aging adds smoke, toast, violet, spices and sawdust.

Grape skin also supplies tannin. A little tannin gives wine structure. Too much has all the charm of a mouthful of stucco. Undrinkably tough young Cabs are often softened up with other grapes. In Bordeaux, the sultan's harem consists of Merlot, Cabernet Franc, Petit Verdot and Malbec. In Australia it's Shiraz and in Italy, Sangiovese.

Tannin, however, is a fabulous preservative, giving Cab the potential for great aging. And here's where it stands head and shoulders above the riff-raff. Just as French Champagne is less about fruit, and more about the remarkable alchemy of yeast and base wine, the miracle of Cabernet is the gorgeous way it evolves in the bottle, turning from fruit into that mysterious thing we call wine.

Back when the occasional ripe harvest was a gift from heaven and enological science consisted of "That's how Grandpa did it," aging was essential. Wine was pretty god-awful without it. Aging is also dandy for the few who can afford to collect or buy older wine.

But how many of us have wine cellars? And if not, why pay a premium for Cab? For some reason, we've always been willing, just as we inexplicably shell out more for Chardonnay than for Pinot Grigio or Sauvignon Blanc. True, there's the extra cost of oak barrels and time spent in them, longer than, say, Merlot. But why pick a wine that needs time in oak to be drinkable in the first place? With so much great wine sold ready-to-drink, does Cab still deserve the crown? Perhaps it's time for a coup d'état, a dethroning or at least a gentle defenestration.

Of course, in the end it comes down to taste: if you love Cabernet, by all means drink it. But you might leave the red carpet at home.

Part 3
Pink, Sweet & Sparkling

FUNNY THING about this category: people love these wines to being with. But then they get all sophisticated and avoid them for years. Eventually they come back, realizing wine can be more than an investment, more than a status symbol; it can also taste really, really good. So, why not just skip the middle step?

PRIMAL FEAR
Pink wine for men, honest

BREASTING THE CROWD like ocean liners through the waves, the women tow bleary-eyed men in striped shirts and crisp navy blazers in their wake. I'm working undercover, pouring wine at the New Orleans Wine Festival. Despite the "Honeys" and "Darlin's" that drip from their lips, women here are clearly the stronger of the species. Maybe that's why they won't touch the rosé.

"Honey, I've moved on to Sauvignon Blanc," says one when I offer her a taste.

"I don't like pink things," says another, "they're not real."

The ones who do taste seem surprised. "It looks like brandy," says one, "But it's refreshing!"

Better writers than I have gone hoarse shouting that news. I could add to the chorus: No, rosé is not red 'n white mixed together. No, it's not sweet and fizzy. Yes, it's food-friendly and every bit as sophisticated, full-flavored and dry as whatever you normally drink.

But why do I have to keep defending it? Why are we so resistant to rosé? Beyond our American wine insecurity, beyond shame-laced memories of white Zin and other sweet fizz, I sense something universal and atavistic about this horror of pink.

Science confirms my suspicions. The field of color psychology studies our reactions to the rainbow around us. This is important if you're selling cars or paint. Despite cultural differences, mostly involving weddings, funerals and luck, many color associations ring true for all societies.

Red, with the longest wavelength, is a power color. It raises the pulse, evoking strength, energy and excitement. At its best, it reads masculine, at its worst, demanding and aggressive, which jibes nicely with the stereotype of the alpha male, drinking big, expensive reds because he can.

White wine is really yellow, an emotional color. It correlates with optimism, confidence and creativity, but an overdose can yield irrationality, anxiety and depression. A unisex color.

Then, oh deary me, there's pink. Blushing flower petals, budding female sexuality, sensitivity, innocence and naïvety are typical associations. "Red with the passion removed," suggests one researcher. Delicacy, tenderness, charm, sweetness and non-violence—the list continues.

Football teams harness this wimp-out factor by painting the visitor's locker room pink. Jails tame fractious prisoners by putting them in Pepto-Bismol colored cells and making them wear pink underwear. And you thought Abu Ghraib was bad.

Too much pink conjures up inhibition, emotional claustrophobia, physical weakness and emasculation. What sort of wine tasting notes could combat that?

A South African producer buffed up his blush by borrowing Champagne's "Blanc de Noirs." Others go with the flow. Le Vin du Cœur, a rosé from Absolut vodka maven Michel Roux, comes with your choice of lovers on the label: a man and a woman, two women or two men.

New Zealand producer Kim Crawford dedicated his rosé to a local drag queen, launching it in a gay bar where guys in pink rubber boots danced on the tables. It's called Pansy.

Try to buck this assault on your id, and another hurdle awaits. Experiments with miscolored food show we're unable to divorce smell and taste from visual cues. Rich-colored drinks taste and smell stronger, even when they're not. Strawberries taste better when they're red instead of blue. A guy's brain might declare a rosé insipid before he's even had a sniff.

Given the scientific basis for pink aversion, how do you explain reams of macho Spaniards, Italians and South American men who swill down the local rosé without the slightest fear of sissiness? Hemingway, for God's sake, knocked back two bottles of Tavel or Spanish rosado a day! And they didn't call him "Papa" for nothing.

Not to mention all the wonderful, male, rosé-drinking American winemakers. Guys who own and operate tuxedos as well as tractors.

Science doesn't always have the last word. Choosing suds over rosé might reassure you that your manhood is intact. But how will you be sure if you can't see it over your beer belly?

JUST DESSERTS
Caressing the bellybutton

"KISSES SWEETER THAN WINE." Ever noticed how many songs and poems equate wine with sweetness? Why is that, when most of the wines we drink are actually pretty dry? And what about that "wine-dark sea" that keeps coming up in *The Odyssey*? Either wine was blue in those days or Homer was having trouble coming up with a metaphor. I can sympathize. In first grade they handed us each a colored pencil and told us to write a poem about it. Things were lower tech, then. My poem began, "Green, it is a wonderful color." Then I got stuck. Finally the perfect solution occurred to me. I continued, "It makes me think of a nice French cruller." Sometimes I still have writing problems like that. But I digress.

Whether your tooth is sweet or not, you can't properly consider wine without considering sugar. The high level of sugar in grapes is what makes wine possible. There are many (no doubt true) stories of the origins of wine, most of them similar to one involving an ancient King Jemseed, who loved grapes so much, he stored them in jars so he'd have them around all year. One day the grapes in one jar weren't sweet anymore. They had fermented. He labeled the spoiled jar "Poison." Seeing this, a lady in his harem who, suffering from seasonal affective disorder, decided to partake and thus end her troubles permanently. But instead of death, she found fun and later, sleep. She woke up feeling much better about everything. Pretty soon the whole court was hooked on "poison." From then on, everyone knew that sugar plus yeast equals buzz.

Winemakers today work carefully to turn all that sugar into alcohol. Usually this takes a week or two. But sometimes it gets stuck, and needs more yeast to get going again. This is how the Sutter Home Winery struck gold. 1972, they were trying to make a dry, full-bodied, white wine from Zinfandel grapes. (Since Zin is a red grape, that means keeping the skins, which contain all the color, out of the batch.) When fermentation stuck, they bottled 26,000 cases of it anyway. It was such a hit that by 1990, white Zin was about a third of all American wine sold, serving as training wheels for countless future wine snobs.

Perhaps for you. But now that you're sophisticated, you drink only dry wine, right? Not so fast. While most table wines are dry, there's a time and place for residual sugar. A slightly sweet, spicy Gewürztraminer, for instance, goes better with Thai or Chinese food than most dry whites. Then there's the whole, heavenly world of dessert wines. These fall into two categories: fortified and natural. Port and sherry are both fortified—beefed up with grape brandy—Port, during fermentation and sherry after. The alcohol in brandy kills yeast and stops fermentation, making most Port and some sherry sweet.

You can also build dessert wine by picking grapes as late as possible, maxed out with sugar. This is risky. Wait too long and you lose the crop to fungus, animals and weather. It's labor intensive, too. Grapes don't mature at exactly the same rate, vines must be picked through daily, with only the ripest grapes selected in each pass.

Trockenbeerenauslese is the highest quality German late harvest wine. *Auslese* means picking out ripe bunches of grapes. *Beeren* means berries, i.e., hand picking separate grapes. *Trocken* means dried, therefore very concentrated sugar. Now say it all together.

Another way to make sweet wine is picking after grapes have frozen on the vine. Pressed while frozen, their water is extruded as shards of ice and what's left is the absolute essence of sweet, heavenly grape-ness. The result is called Eiswein in Germany, and ice wine in Canada, where it's becoming as important and reliable an export for them as hockey players. You can fake all this by putting the grapes in a freezer, but the results are desultory—none of the depth of flavor, or zingy liveliness that keeps sweet wines from cloying.

Despite ole Jemseed's experience, good sweet wines take a lot of work. Leave the tiniest bit of yeast in the bottle, and a new fermentation might start, turning the wine dry and probably fizzy. Which is how Champagne was discovered. But that's another story, about another king, for another day.

LIQUID GOLD
From fuzz to nectar

"I DO NOT LIKE GREEN EGGS AND HAM! I will not eat them, Sam-I-Am!" The words of Dr. Seuss flashed through my mind when Xavier Planty, winemaker at Château Giraud in the Sauternes appellation of Bordeaux, handed me a bunch of shriveled, moldy grapes. Put something gray and furry in my mouth? Not in a box or on a train or with a fox or in the rain. But when I finally screwed up the courage, they were surprisingly delicious. And when I tasted the wine they made, I was in heaven. The wine is Sauternes, and the fur, *botrytis cinerea*.

There are sweet wines, and then there's Sauternes. The ultimate belly button wine, its mouth-feel is thick, almost viscous. The color ranges from butter to saffron to amber, and the luscious bouquet can include honeysuckle, creamsicle, nuts and apricots. Made from Sauvignon Blanc and Semillon grapes, this wine can age almost indefinitely. In fact, hundred-year-old bottles have a complex nuttiness you can't find in younger wine. The price of this luxury is bracingly high, but unlike some cases of niche marketing run amok, with Sauternes there's a good reason. Mold.

The vignerons of Sauternes grovel at the feet of a microscopic mushroom that occasionally deigns to descend and suck the life out of their grapes. Fastening on and digging in with sharp needles, it drains the grapes of water and acids, turning the fruit into a concentrated bomb of sugar and heady flavor.

The Mushroom God extracts a price. It demands the rare microclimate of hot sun, plus a cool morning mist. Only the ripest grapes are affected, so the harvest must wait, and wait, while growers pray and bite their nails, knowing that the advent of rain and cold will destroy everything. If the mold does come, it attacks unevenly. The pickers have to pass through the vines over and over, hand-selecting the grottiest grapes each time.

What usually takes a couple of days takes weeks in Sauternes. Next, a substantial sacrifice at the altar. A viticultural rule of thumb has it that each vine produces a bottle of wine. At Château d'Yquem, the high shrine of Sauternes, each vine yields only one glass.

Thinking in terms of tithing to this temple will soften the blow on your pocketbook a little. Happily, too, Sauternes doesn't have a total monopoly on these growing conditions. The so-called *noble* rot shows up in other parts of France and Germany on a variety of white grapes. You can learn more at www.sapros.org, but be prepared for a disarming dose of religious fervor.

Some day, no doubt, America will have its own version, but gods are not cultivated quickly.

Rather than drink it with dessert, drink it *as* dessert. You wouldn't eat a banana split while taking communion, would you? It's also appropriate as an aperitif, when you can give it your full attention, and it's classically mated with foie gras.

But I don't suppose there's any time I'd kick it out of bed. At Château Giraud, I shared lunch with the grape pickers and their children at long trestle tables under a shed. We ate lamb stew and mussels in broth sopped up with hunks of crusty bread.

Winemaker Planty kept my glass filled with fresh, young, lemon-meringue-pie Sauternes, and believe me, it all went down just fine. Not only had my disgust at the furry fungus subsided, I was certain that I would drink it here or there—why, I would drink it anywhere! I felt like giving him a hug and saying, "Thank you, thank you, Sam-I-Am." But that would have been a little weird.

THAT THING IN THE CELLAR
The mystery of Tokaj

YOU'VE SEEN THOSE WINE CELLARS with travertine counters, cleverly interlocking zebra-wood racks, and age-tracking software. All that money could go into wine! Don't they get it? It's a cellar! You know, as in cell? It's for roots and coal, spiders and snakes. This is where you lock bad children. Pity the naughty little wine snoblings, reduced to screaming, "Let me out, Mommy! There's white Zinfandel in here!"

Europe does cellars right; ancient, dank caves where you don't need the aim of William Tell to spit. One Old World winemaker lifted a hatch in his cellar floor and showed me shrimp swimming around, inches below our feet. Talk about damp! Another cellar had a foot of mold covering the walls and ceilings. In it, glimmering randomly like mosaics at Ravenna, were coins from every era. I pulled a Euro out of my pocket and pushed it into the black sponge and there it stuck, right next to an ancient Roman *denarius*.

The caves of Champagne are a maze of chalk tunnels, like a colony for effervescent termites. I know a restaurant with an underwater cellar; you order wine and they send a diver down for it. But the most mysterious, fascinating cellars of all are in the Tokaj-Hegyalja region of Hungary, home of the mythical, sweet, Tokaji Aszú wine.

Long before the Rhine and Sauternes, since at least 1571, Hungary has been spinning mold into gold, letting the fuzzy fingers of *botrytis cinerea* shrivel grapes to where they yield but one glass per vine. But such a glass!

In a good year, the first few drops become Eszencia, a kind of scummy pond sludge too sweet to drown in, and so rare they sell it by the spoonful in Hungarian restaurants for the equivalent of $19 a sip. At less than 3 percent alcohol, it's not so much wine as highly revered bodily fluid. When it's not being worshipped it's blended into Aszú.

Grapes are next milled into paste and dumped by the bucket, or *puttonyo*, into a base wine, which starts them fermenting. The current fashion is minimal aging in barrels kept brimfull to prevent oxidation. This "Sauternes style" wine is pale gold, flowery-soft and creamy. Delicious, certainly, but a far cry from the storied stuff that Louis XIV called "King of wine and wine of kings," and that Napoleon III's wife, Eugénie, credited for her girlish complexion at the age of 94. Still, it's far better than 16 years ago, when communists were apt to disguise plonk by instant-aging with oxidation as well as subjecting it to fortifying, pasteurization and other indignities too brutal to mention.

Now, traditionalists are reviving the real Tokaji Aszú, unique and unearthly. As wine writer Hugh Johnson put it, "There's something going on in those cellars."

And it's in the walls. Traditional Tokaji ferments for a couple of years (compared to days for most table wines), as well as aging in cellars of volcanic rock—cold, damp tunnels, up to 20 miles long. Their walls are covered in microflora like no place else on earth: microbes, yeast, bacteria and over fifty species of fungus. This mold creeps down to blanket everything in sight, including bottles, barrels and the surface of fermenting wine. Though barrels are neither full nor tightly stoppered, no oxygen gets in.

During this process, called *darabbantartás*, strange things happen. Sugars caramelize, not because of heat, but because amino acids break down, turning the wine from gold to amber. The breakdown of glutamic acid infuses the wine with umami, the savory fifth taste embodied in sautéed mushrooms and soy sauce. This adds an overall tang, plus distinct notes of dark rye bread.

Even more than red wine, old-school Tokaji is a pharmacy of health products. Polyamines and nitrogenous compounds promote cell metabolism and the synthesis of RNA, DNA and protein. It's also crammed with antioxidants including resveratrol, vitamin E and superoxide-dismustaste (SOD), which, variously prevent cancer and dementia, lower blood pressure, and foster good skin tone, like the empress said.

All this, and a taste like heaven. They have rye bread in heaven, don't they? So next time you get the urge to clean your basement—put down that mop! Sometimes grottiness is next to godliness.

TONGS FOR THE MEMORIES
How to win friends and decapitate people

SAVOIR FAIRE—you can't even pronounce it. You pull corks with the dexterity of a walrus and regard the wine list as a third rail. But here's your chance to corner a bit of wine suave where even snobs are shaky. With a little study, even you could become The Pasha of Port.

Yes, Port. The name reeks of velvet smoking jackets (you'd look good in a smoking jacket), of blazing stone hearths and rows of faded ancestors. It puts color in the cheeks and courage in the heart. And what a comfort on these long winter nights when global warming has forsaken us.

The potion from Portugal is an English invention. Back in the 18th century, Brits relied on a steady stream of French wine to help them forget they lived in damp castles and drove on the wrong side of the road. The crafty French pounced on this weakness during one of their regularly scheduled wars. They turned off the faucet, thus winning the battle at the expense of a lot of wine sales, an economic policy they continue to favor today. Desperate Brits searching for their fix discovered that Portugal had lovely vineyards, too. Unfortunately, they made wretched wine, but the Anglos were too sick of beer to care.

To keep the wines from spoiling on the voyage up the

coast, they included in their wine making a dollop of brandy as preservative. To their delighted surprise, the extra alcohol halted fermentation partway through, leaving a deliciously sweet wine that became a British staple for the next 200 years.

Hear that bell? Time to gather up our History books and move down the hall to Chemistry for a brief overview of categories of Port. These are worth the trouble of memorizing in order to intimidate your friends.

Vintage Port is made of grapes from a single harvest, and only in exceptional years. It's bottled early and then requires decades of aging to reach its prime.

Late Bottled Vintage is a nice alternative if you're broke or impatient. Kept in wood a bit longer, it delivers an approximation of the vintage experience without all that cash and waiting.

Ruby Port goes quickly from barrel to bottle. It's meant to be young, dark red and intensely fruity.

Tawny Port spends anywhere from six to over 100 years in oak and then emerges nutty and brown, oozing flavors of toffee, caramel and vanilla. The older it gets the more delicate, pale and expensive it will be.

But amortize the costs. Thanks to the preservative effect of all that alcohol and sugar, Port is one of the few wines you can uncork and keep drinking for weeks: as an aperitif, a dessert wine or a shot to steady the nerves before a harrowing task like trying to get live tech support on the phone.

Port is shot through with the rituals and initiations of a particularly British obsession: keeping others out. Usually of one's club, an exclusive refuge where one asserts one's supremacy by substituting "one" for "you" or "me," thereby avoiding the faux pas of actually committing to a concrete statement. The initiated know that Port is always passed from right to left. Should your host ask if you're acquainted with the Bishop of Norwich, it's code for: The bottle ran aground in front of you ten minutes ago, man! For God's sake, pass it on.

But for the slickest ritual of all, try Port Tongs. After fifty years or more, a cork can get crumbly. Rather than shred it with a corkscrew, you (or one) brandish(es) a pair of long iron calipers with wooden handles. Stick the metal ends in the fire until they're red-hot. Then clamp them around the neck of the bottle, just below the bottom of the cork. After a minute or two, to be enlivened with Houdini-like gestures of danger and mystery, remove the tongs, hand them to an assistant, and quickly wrap the bottle neck in a cold, wet napkin. The sudden change of temperature will cause the glass to break neatly and the neck and cork to come off in your hand.

That's what's supposed to happen, anyway. Other possibilities involve third degree burns and glass shards flying around the room. It might be a good idea to wear safety goggles, and practice a few times before trying to impress, say, an OSHA inspector.

With many long nights of Port-fueled practice, your prowess will grow. You might even invent an arcane ritual of your own. Guaranteed to impress one's friends. Frightfully.

THE SWORD & THE BUBBLE
Champagne: To savor and saber

MY COUSIN CHRISTIAN, who wields a mean saber, has decapitated some 200 bottles of bubbly. Done correctly, the procedure involves impressive flourishes, as well as dubious historical tales of galloping Cossacks and jokes about performing a bris. Most important, though, is that the bottle be Champagne.

Champagne has more bubbles than other sparkling wine— according to Bollinger Champagne "fizzicist" Tom Stevenson, around 250 million little pearls of CO_2. When the top is whacked off, bubble pressure shoots both neck and cork across the room, hopefully not into someone's soup or cleavage, although Christian says that happens. Too little pressure and you risk glass dropping into the bottle. Higher pressure also dictates thicker bottle glass, which breaks off more cleanly than thinner stuff. So after a few desultory attempts on foreign bottles, he will only wield the sword with real Champagne.

That's also why it's a good thing that in December, 2000, a British couple had bottles of Bollinger, not some stateside crud, in their drinks refrigerator when a fire broke out. According to *Decanter* magazine, they were woken by the sound of popping corks and came downstairs to find their fridge aflame. But luckily, heat was bursting the corks out of the bottles inside and since carbon dioxide starves fire of oxygen, the froth of Champagne doused the flames.

While we all love Champagne for its fire retardant properties, it's also just plain fun. It makes you feel good, thanks to festive associations as well as chemistry: It increases testosterone, raises blood alcohol faster and keeps you more buoyant, longer.

Besides, bubbles are simply cool. Sparkling wine is the grownup version of Pop Rocks. And pops for the same reason: CO_2, yearning to be free. They add it to the molten candy at 600 pounds per square inch where it forms tiny, high-pressure bubbles that burst when the little pellets melt in your mouth.

Getting the bubbles into Champagne is a little harder. They start with austere, highly acidic, still wine and blend up to seventy different batches to make the perfect *cuvée*. This is infused with yeast and sugar and put into super-strong bottles which are sealed with a bottle cap and put down to rest. A second fermentation takes place inside the bottle, producing CO_2, and hence, bubbles. This takes about a month, but the bottles lie there another two to four years, deriving complexity from the yeast, which forms a gunky residue that has to be removed. This is done in three steps:

1. **Riddling:** Bottles go onto a special rack at a slight

angle, neck-down. Every day, for 12 weeks, each one is picked up, given a shake to loosen residue and rotated one-eighth of a turn. The angle is gradually increased until the bottle is almost upside-down and all the yeast is gathered in the neck. There are machines for this, but most is still done by hand in traditional wineries where carpal tunnel syndrome runs rampant.

2. Dégorgement: The neck of the bottle is plunged into a subfreezing bath. As the cap is removed, built-up pressure from carbon dioxide shoots out a plug of frozen sediment. This must be done quickly and carefully so as not to lose pressure, wine or an eye.

3. Dosage: An elixir of sugar, wine, and sometimes brandy is added, determining the sweetness and style of the resulting Champagne. Then the bottle is quickly corked and ages a few months more before going to market.

Even without a sword, opening Champagne is dangerous. The pressure inside is three times what's in your car tires. The higher the altitude, the more the bubbles yearn to be free. Wrap a napkin around the bottle, point it away from anything of value, and gently turn the bottle as you ease the cork out. The quieter the pop, the less you'll spill.

Most Champagne is made to be drunk quickly, not aged. Refrigerate what you don't finish. Even uncorked, it will stay effervescent for days; cold keeps the bubbles in solution.

So, don't wait for romance to open a bottle. Nine out of ten fizzicists recommend you pop that cork tonight!

Part 4
Components

WE'RE ALMOST READY TO TASTE. Careful—send your nose in alone, it will probably report back something profound like, "Um…wine." It's not your nose's fault. It needs backup. Namely, your brain. Equipped with a map of components.

Components are the building blocks of wine: acid, earth and wood, tannin, fruit and sugar. Learn what they mean and how to recognize them, you'll be ready for anything the tasting situation can throw you.

THE STING
Acid and balance

IT'S A DECENT LITTLE SUSHI JOINT; still, we have to wedge a coaster under one leg to keep the table from going ka-chunk when we lean on it. My friend Richard orders iced green tea. He takes a sip, and then says to the waitress, "I know this is probably wrong, but could you bring me some sweetener?"

But it's *exactly* right! The tea is high in tannin and acid—he knows instinctively that sugar would complete the balance. In wine, "balance" sounds like an esoteric concept like Feng Shui or Sinn Fein—I get them mixed up—the sort of thing that only people with more finely tuned sensibilities than yours can appreciate. Actually, it's as simple and instinctive as mixing iced tea.

Or wedging a wobbly table. Except instead of legs to even up you've got components, like oak, tannin, sugar and alcohol. And just as important, toiling away in the background like so many munchkins on meth, are the acids.

If tannin is wine's backbone, acid is its nervous system. If tannin frames the house, acid wires it for electricity. If tannin plays bass, acid is the string section

You're familiar with acid if you ever noticed the walls breathing in and out and leaves on the wallpaper turn into insects and begin crawling up the…oh, wait, wrong acid. Here we go; the main acids in wine are as follows:

Tartaric adds body and tartness. Eventually, it forms crystals that drop out of the liquid; you've probably seen them at the bottom of a bottle or stuck to the cork. They won't hurt you any more than that jar of white stuff that's been on your spice rack all these years: cream of tartar. It's essentially the scrapings from the inside of wine barrels. I've never figured out what you're supposed to do with it. Maybe the people who sell sets of spices needed something to even up the row: "Make it white, Roger. It'll set off the chervil."

Malic tastes like green apples. Too much tastes as sharp as old Granny Smith's tongue, so many whites and virtually all reds undergo *malolactic* fermentation, which transforms it into much mellower lactic acid, the kind in milk and cream. Lactic is the buttered popcorn you find wedged in the overstuffed cushions of some American Chardonnay.

Citric acid is the lemon-lime-grapefruit squirt that livens up certain whites and rosés. Not much of it occurs naturally in grapes, so sometimes it's added for zing.

Succinic is the best acid you never heard of; a salty-sour-bitter flavor common to everything fermented.

Those are the good guys, the fixed acids. Then there's *acetic* acid, called "volatile" because it boils away at low temperatures. A smidgeon brings out aromas and flavors, but beyond that you get nose-wrinkling odors of vinegar and nail polish remover.

Acid affects how other components taste. Enough lemons turn sugar water into lemonade. Champagne and young German Rieslings are surprisingly crammed with sugar, but high acid makes them seem dry.

Ever complained about a wine that ate the rust right off your bumper, only to be told "But it's a *food* wine!"? Well, yeah, it's an excuse, but often it's true. Low-acid sipping wines, voluptuous and soft, smooth and sweet, are solo players. While the ensemble work of dinner is a job for the high-acid wine. Acid makes you salivate. It freshens your palate between bites, making food taste better and go down easier. Higher-acid wines taste cleaner, more refreshing, sharper, fruitier and drier.

Acid, along with tannin and sugar, is a preservative—a crucial ingredient in any wine destined for aging. Some grape varieties naturally have more than others. Riesling and Barbera ring in high, while Viognier, Marsanne and Gewürztraminer score low. Whites usually have more than reds and dessert wines the most of all.

Young grapes and cool climates produce the highest acid. As grapes ripen, acid levels go down. Warm climates *can* produce lively acid if the nights are cool. In Napa, for instance. In a region like Tuscany, though, where sweat never sleeps, jangling acids just ain't going to happen.

Your stomach lining has a say as well. Some people are acutely sensitive to the burn of acid while others notice nothing.

High or low is a question of situation and taste. It's not about picking one style but about balance, i.e., knowing which leg to saw off if your wine goes ka-chunk.

DISHING THE DIRT
What's earth doing in my glass?

WHEN I GET OFF A PLANE IN EUROPE, something smells different, distinctly European. It takes a moment to register what it is: people. They don't smell in America. Oh, sure, the occasional heavy smoker or gutter-dweller telegraphs his presence quite clearly. What's missing here is the normal smell of bodies, vibrant and strangely pleasant, like someone had turned up the warm tones on the color monitor of life. It's hard to find an American who doesn't take a shower at least once a day— twice if he does anything sweaty—and it's hard to find a European who does.

I wonder if this cultural subtext explains a wine issue that also divides along the Euro-American fault line: earth. When you taste blind, earthiness (or lack thereof) is a major clue to a wine's origin. Wines from the Old World mostly have it; wines from the New World seldom do.

The term *earth* is pretty broad. It encompasses, for instance, the category of minerals. Petrol and diesel are easy to smell in older German Riesling, but *slate*, a term often used for the younger sort, is elusive. I've ruined more than one emperor's fashion show by pointing out that rocks don't smell. I'm usually told to think about rocks *after they'd been rained on*. Chalk baffles me, too. Chablis is sometimes described as chalky, and there's talk of "dusty, chalky aromas." When I read about "smooth, chalky raspberry and cherry flavors," I'm not sure if they're describing rosé or Robitussin.

Mostly, though, *earth* means something organic—truffles, topsoil or leaves rotting on the forest floor. If you can't quite wrap your nose around *bramble*, how about a heaving pile of composting mulch? Dust and cobwebs describe the drier side of earth.

Where do these flavors and aromas come from? I have yet to meet the winemaker who doesn't claim the soils of his vineyard are mirrored in his wine. Flinty wines from flinty fields, chalk from chalk, and the club-soda-like minerality of gneiss and loess from their respective alluvial beds. Whether this reflects heartfelt belief or merely a clever profit/loess statement, scientists dispute the concept.

Research in Australia, California and Europe suggests earthiness is a result of clonal selection and that if soil composition has anything to do with it at all, it's not the mineral content but the soil's capacity to retain or drain water that makes a difference.

The lion's share of earthiness comes from *brettanomyces*, a wild yeast that can both bless and curse a winery. When it comes, it doesn't just pay a visit—it unpacks its pajamas and toothbrush and moves in for good. Almost all red wines have a trace of brett. At low levels it adds complexity. You can thank it for the traditional regional characters of the finest from the Rhône, Burgundy and Bordeaux. Besides earth, its tang also evokes game, bacon, leather and mushrooms.

Some people—especially squeaky-clean, well-showered Americans who prefer their wines fruity—consider it a fault. Their vocabulary for brett includes barnyard, wet dog, stale hamburger, sweaty horse blanket, Band-Aid and chicken droppings. And everyone agrees that too much brett overwhelms fruit and renders wine revoltingly undrinkable.

Yet the sort of wine that sends shivers up and down the spines of enophiles is inevitably earthy. Why should this be? Think of dirty as the opposite of bland. If you're squeamish about what's gross, you'll miss a lot of pleasure.

Think of a wild crush you had, preferably someone who broke your heart. What image brings back that familiar stab of pain and/or pleasure? Abs of steel? A perfect set of Miss America Chiclets? I doubt it. More likely something unique: mussed-up hair, a certain freckle, an attitude. A mole becomes a beauty mark when it punctuates a face of mathematically-bland perfection. In the same way, earthy oddness that cannot be manufactured in the winery balances the correct flavors that can. Think of earth as wine's birthmark, the thumbprint not of its maker but of its Maker.

CLUNK OUT THE BARREL
The good, the bad and the oakly

IS NOTHING SACRED? Thanks to Switzerland's Cybox Company, we now have the square wine barrel. I guess it was bound to happen. Traditional barrel shapes were doomed the day France adopted the metric system and couldn't figure out how many hogsheads to the deciliter.

Barrels have been getting a bad rap lately, what with some Chardonnays having more in common with the dining room table than the food upon it. More and more wines are proudly proclaiming their un-oaked status.

In some cases this is a slightly disingenuous selling point, along the lines of: CORNFLAKES—NOW 100% SNAIL-FREE! Some wines, in fact, have always eschewed wood. Others are only aged there after fermenting in steel. Still others are fermented and aged in the same oak barrel, a bit like my high school where we took sex- and drivers-ed in the same car.

Long before they were a seasoning, barrels were high-tech storage and mailing units, far less breakable than amphorae. A fortuitous side effect was evaporation: As water and alcohol leave, flavor concentrates. Other chemical reactions affect texture, making wine rounder and lusher in the mouth.

Balsamic vinegar passes through a rainbow of different woods, but so far only a few species of white oak work for wine. For a while, only French oak could cut it. Early American barrels, made by whiskey coopers, had desultory results. The looser grain of American oak, plus the fact that whiskey staves were sawed rather than split like French planks, put more wood surface in contact with the wine. Another difference was that French coopers dry their planks outside for at least 24 months, while Americans, in their perpetual hurry, used a kiln. Two years of wind and rain changes wood chemicals considerably. When American coopers started copying French methods, their barrels became respectable, though they retain a distinctly different accent. As do barrels from Hungary, Poland and wherever else oak is grown.

Searing barrels over fire was originally done to seal wood fibers and strengthen the staves. Nowadays, winemakers order light, medium or heavy toast for the flavors they impart, although this doesn't work quite the way you might think. For instance, new studies show that more charring results in *less* smokiness in the wine.

The flavor wars escalated. Since oak goes neutral after a few years of use, wineries began using more and more new wood. You'll even see claims of "200% New Oak," made possible by racking wine out of one series of brand-new barrels and into another.

The spicy-sweet vanilla and brash coconut aromas from oak can, and often do, cover a world of sins; the chief one being weak, flavorless wine. We Americans happily lap up these oak-shakes. The rest of the world blames our national sweet tooth. A natural result, they assert, of our parents having filled our baby bottles with Coke (instead of beer, like I've seen them do in Germany). They suspect some of our more patriotic nursing mothers actually lactate Pepsi.

I have a different theory: for a brief, shining moment, oak simplified things. Compared to exotica like "white stone-fruit" and "bramble," the whiff of vanilla was easy to recognize. Better yet, it was a seal of approval: a guarantee of high-quality wine.

But the riff raff went and ruined it. They flooded the market with fakes: Subway-vendor Rolex wines that tasted like they'd been in expensive oak barrels, but hadn't. This is accomplished by tossing in oak beans, oak chips, oak extract and nylon-mesh teabags full of oak shavings. Other foak remedies include staves that float up and fan out and the mysterious oak matrix; all available in French, American, Hungarian or Polish wood; single, double, treble-toasted or raw.

Another rule of thumb, whacked off at the knuckle. So here we are again, out in the wilderness with no compass and only our palates to guide us. It's tempting to do the trendy thing and eschew anything that ever touched a tree. But then you'd be missing some amazing complexity that purely fruit-driven wines can't begin to approach.

Not to mention a chance to taste history. The very last tree from an oak forest planted by Louis XIV to supply timber for navy ships just sold to a Bordeaux cooper for $45,600. Planted in 1669, Le Chêne de Morat is 40 meters high and 15 feet around and should yield about 60 barrels after they fell it this spring. Now I'd give my matrix for a taste of that.

AND YOU CAN'T MAKE ME
Hard-wired preferences

HAVE YOU EVER FED A TWO-YEAR-OLD, or been one? Then you're familiar with the old "Open the hangar and in flies aero-spoon!" maneuver. I never fell for it. I realized quite early if I closed my mouth tight, no one could put another spoonful of creamed spinach in there as long as I lived.

Which is not to say that people haven't tried. At wine tasting dinners I'm often plied, for instance, with cheese, which I don't happen to eat. Whether this is because I'm a) lactose intolerant, b) health conscious, or c) a founding member of the Bacterial Rights Movement, is hardly relevant. Yet my refusal doesn't sit well, and people continue to push. I simply *must* try this Stilton with the Port.

People are quite certain what *ought* to give you pleasure, whether the realm is cars, music, clothing or wine. As a social creature, you might find yourself caving to the pressure, even though when you're all alone you switch PBS to *Elimidate*, and swap Camus for FHM.

Day after day, like a priest, I receive the shamefaced confessions of penitents admitting to the sin of liking sweet wine. Of course their spouse is right; they've got to get beyond this hang-up and into the realm of serious, dry reds. As though tuning into wine mystique were an item to cross off the to-do list: take down the Christmas wreath, drop the clothes off at Goodwill, and get over those bottles of infantile, pink fizz.

This is so topsy-turvy. For one thing, the spouse is off-base. Sweet, pink and fizzy are all…cool! Don't believe me? Go to the best restaurant you can afford—the kind where wine is displayed in a twelve-story ice-cave and trained polar bears shimmy up the walls to retrieve your order. Ask the sommelier to recommend a rosé, a semi-sweet white, a gloppy dessert wine, or even the trifecta: sweet, pink *and* fizzy. Does the man in white scoff so hard he spews in his silver ashtray? Hardly! He *loves* these wines! He thought you'd never ask. And he understands immediately that you, and not your status-bound spouse, are the real taster.

But suppose we give the benefit of the doubt to your significant other, who might be advocating from a true, sensual love of certain wines and just wants you to see the light. Nice, but still misguided.

Here's why. I don't like the rug pulled out from under me, and wine is a master of this trick. I fight back by taking detailed tasting notes so I can accurately recall a wine whether I tasted it in moonlight as the winemaker held it to my lips and whispered sweet sales pitches in my ear, or in the neon light of a physics lab with a nerd whispering dry chemical formulas.

But even the best notes can be foiled by your own, personal chemistry. In sickness and in health, medicated or stone cold sober, sweating or shivering, sleepy or buzzed—all of these states and more can totally change your perception. Immune to my obsessive note taking, a white might scour like Brillo one week, and go down like lemonade on a hot summer's day the next. Velvety, generous reds can go tarry and bitter, only to resume the seduction a few weeks, months or flu seasons later.

When it happens in your own mouth, it's easy to grasp how profoundly different wine might taste to someone else. Debating "red" with your spouse might be as relevant as arguing "green" with the colorblind.

Next time you feel pressure to like the "right" wine, respect your own, personal palate. Foil stupid debates by buying half bottles, or each ordering what you want by the glass. Know that if things get ugly, the sommelier will cover your back. Finally, when all else fails, shut down the hangar and make the airplane detour to Detroit.

Part 5
Tasting

WINE-TASTING IS FUN TO PARODY, because from the outside it just seems so preposterous. Kind of like square-dancing: at first, a bunch of morons hopscotching around in petticoats and lederhosen—you wouldn't be caught dead doing that! But then, one day, you try it. And darn it all if you aren't just having heaps of fun! So dust off your dirndle, shave your knees and let's start tasting.

GRAPE EXPECTATIONS
Quit thinking so hard

I'M COMING DOWN off a pretty ugly karaoke experience, so cut me some slack. Yeah, I know you're supposed to look like an idiot up there, but this was different. It wasn't just that I sounded like a bagpipe in labor. Or that the audience formed an action committee to have me recalled. The problem is that I was once a fairly decent singer; I'm talking musical theater, nightclubs, even opera. So people who had heard me had *expectations.* Not at all the case for my friend Jill, who, one night after a few vodka tonics ("And I probably had some shots," she adds), belted her way through "Hey Mickey," and finished by falling backward off the stage.

Expectations can ruin the wine experience. Pity the

would-be gentleman who expects to handle wine duties with James Bondian panache. Especially if he reads the glossy men's magazines that regularly run advice on wine savvy alongside strategies for tipping, choosing an alpha-male sound system and talking a woman out of her clothes. The truth is, very few people are fluent in wine-list these days. A generation ago, it was enough to be able to pronounce *Pouilly-Fuissé*. Now that we're inundated with excellent wine from every corner of the earth, it's impossible to keep up unless you make it your life's work. If you're smart, you ask for help. That's what the sommelier and wine store guys are for.

I twigged to this at 19, in Paris. My American boyfriend had just finished a wine-tasting class. Eager to use his new expertise, he took me to dinner at a restaurant with white tablecloths and smirking waiters. Shaking only a little, he plunged bravely into the wine list and came up with the one red he could decode. When it arrived, though, it was white. I didn't want to humiliate him, and he wasn't admitting he screwed up, so we both pretended it was what we wanted, and drank it.

Pros get bogged down by expectations, too. That's why they do blind tastings. Wouldn't you be just a tad more forgiving if you knew the faded, tasteless stuff in your glass was over-the-hill Hermitage, not top-of-the-line Bud's Garage?

Sometimes our expectations are simply stupid. Eight wines into a vaguely professional tasting at Flora Springs Winery in Napa, someone described a Sauvignon Blanc as "grassy," with notes of "peach and gooseberry." The rest of us nodded in agreement as we sloshed, gurgled and spit. After a moment, winery president John Komes said, "Has anyone ever even seen a gooseberry?" Silence. "Or tasted one?" We shook our heads. Apparently, we had all read a lot of reviews and come to expect this taste to be described as "gooseberry." Or we were all lying. Either way, for all we knew, gooseberries didn't even exist.

We discussed starting a stealth campaign. We'd plant news items about an emperor's new berry. "Aggressive green-apple notes," we might write, "with hints of dried *leürgenberry* on the mid-palate." How long would that take to spread? Who would have the guts to challenge it?

Expecting wine to be consistent without accounting for context is a recipe for disappointment. A bottle of Condrieu that drinks like nectar at a candlelit table with the crush of your life licking their lips and telling you you're the most desirable creature on the planet loses some charm when drunk during a dishwasher unloading. Ditto the Amarone you sampled from the barrel at that ancient winery tucked in the hills of the Veneto. Back in the suburbs, the "exotic dried plum character" just tastes like prunes.

In wine and most other things, I try to stick with a philosophy I learned from my brother-in-law, Ludwig: Whatever it is you're awaiting—*expect a deli sandwich*. No more, no less. A deli sandwich is never unwelcome. On the pain-to-pleasure scale, it falls on the positive side of neutral, somewhere between clean socks and an all-expense-paid trip to Tahiti. If you get something better, whoopee! If not, no sweat. Incidentally, on that scale? I'd put karaoke right between "toilet backing up" and "eaten by a shark."

THE NOSE KNOWS
More than you, anyway

"YOUR LAST COLUMN, with all its flavors, fruits and nuts made me wonder," writes my father. "I can never sniff out those things." He echoes many who suspect that tasting notes are just for wine writers—a communication akin to the elephant's stomp echoing across the savannah over subsonic wavelengths, or the dolphin's screech, picked up by cetaceans hundreds of miles away. "Hark!" they imagine us saying, "Someone mentioned 'hints of Asian red pear on the finish.' It must be one of my species, with whom I could mate and produce fertile, pretentious offspring!"

My father is a musician. I could tell him that sometimes when I listen to a symphony all I hear is music—none of those D-flats, minor-sevenths and tempi changes he talks about. In both cases the lack is not equipment, but training and intent. You can appreciate wine without a sophisticated nose. Even highly-trained European wine professionals tend to talk more about mouth-feel and less about aromas.

Still, stopping to smell the rosé is fascinating. Your tongue can taste only five properties: sweet, sour, bitter, salt and the savory thing called umami. Of those, salt is very seldom a component in wine. Flavors, actually, depend highly on your sense of smell. Apart from the sensory pleasure of color, clarity and perhaps even price, everything else is up to your nose.

And your nose is up to it. Our sensitivity to smells is astonishing. We can detect the off odor of hydrogen sulfide (rotten eggs) in concentrations of three parts per billion. That's like stumbling upon one particular family of three in China. There is a bell-pepper aroma in Cabernet Sauvignon that we can make out at concentrations of one to five parts per *trillion*. Sort of like finding a one-cent error in your 10 billion dollar checking account.

If you want to be a smarty-pants, smells from the grape are called *aroma* while smells from winemaking, such as fermentation, lees or oak-aging, are called *bouquet*.

Some of these odors are detected by sniffing. But if you stick your nose in and come up with nothing, take heart. You get two more chances with the retro-nasal route—your nose's back door. First, when the wine's in your mouth, which accounts for the licorice, hazelnut or banana you may think you're "tasting." Second, when you swallow and exhale, known as the finish.

The Wine Aroma Wheel lists and categorizes smells ranging from *diesel* to *wet dog* to *soy sauce*. The idea is to standardize the description of odors. It contains 135 odors, but those are only the ones we have words for. Most people can be trained to identify around a thousand different smells and wine is estimated to contain at least 200 of them.

Alas, your nose can be a traitor: brilliant sleuth one day, on strike when you need it. It helps to keep it in shape. You can learn a lot by smelling around your own garden and spice rack, as well as the supermarket produce section. That way you begin to find your personal blind spots. At the Riedel crystal factory in Austria, I sniffed my way down a row of twenty opaque-black glasses, each containing a wine component such as chocolate, thyme or blackberries. Leather and plums were a snap, but even the third time through I couldn't get black pepper or apricots.

There are also nose kits, collections of little vials of wine-related scent. Do they work? Mine taught me what "acacia" smells like, though I've yet to run across it in wine. I had to banish the thing to the garage when grapefruit essence took over the house. Kits of wine faults like oxidized, cooked and corked, teach you to send wine back with aplomb, but beware: Those chemicals can camp out in your nose for days.

Because smells pass directly from your nose to your limbic system, bypassing the reasoning parts of your brain, they can evoke strong emotions. You might become suddenly sad, well before consciously noticing your ex-girlfriend's perfume wafting by.

Advertisers are working hard to exploit this phenomenon. Soon to come: odor dispensers for your computer, capable of scent-blending feats akin to turning four colors of ink into a rainbow. Gamers will get the added nasal dimension of burnt rubber tires, gun powder and blood. You'll be able to sample, blend and order perfume right at your desk. On-line wine schools will command your computer to puff out Syrah and Merlot, so you can learn the difference. Online stores will do their best to seduce you, betting that the right aroma could have you clicking the shopping cart icon before your inner accountant has even sharpened his pencil.

The technology is already at work, dispensing Tyrannosaurus breath, frankincense and Roman soldier's armpit at museum exhibits, zippy, citric blends in offices, and calming lavender in subways. Nostalgic scents from the1920s are even arousing Alzheimer's patients in nursing homes.

As for wine, how about improving jug juice by inhaling computer-generated Grand Cru Bordeaux as you sip? Or the aroma could come from the package. There are now Styrofoam containers that release odors of the food within when microwaved.

MRIs—the shelf-stable hunks of dehydrated cardboard we feed our soldiers—are getting a makeover: eau-de-chipped-beef will be embedded in the fabric of the bag. So why not a wine bottle that wafts Cab when uncorked? Or glasses embedded with the unmistakable terroir scent of Burgundy and Alsace?

I love to imagine the possibilities, while drinking—not analyzing—a glass of wine. Once in a while you've got to put down the pen and just let the wine and music carry you away.

TRIAL BY TASTE
Are you a super-taster?

CAN YOU SEPARATE oak tannins from seed tannins in a single sip? Know whether that's tartaric or citric acid prickling your tongue? Find some wines undrinkably bitter or sharp, while those around you drink on unaware? Well, I hope you look good in tights, because you may be a super-taster. If you can't do those things, don't toss the ThighMaster yet. You might still have super powers; but it takes training to unleash them.

In experiments dating to the 1930s, scientists defined three categories of taste perception. Fifty percent of the population are tasters. They perceive flavors in a normal way. Twenty-five percent are non-tasters and miss out on a lot, while the other twenty-five percent are super-tasters.

Prepare to accept your lot. How well you taste is determined genetically. Researchers can classify you using a chemical called PROP (6-N-propylthiouracil). Non-tasters can't distinguish it from water. Tasters perceive it as bitter, while super-tasters find it so revolting they gag, retch and usually quit the study.

You'd think super-tasting would make food and drink a garden of delights. Surely it describes the chefs and gourmands of the world. Actually, the talent is not all pleasant. Super-tasters find sweets twice as sweet and bitter foods twice as bitter. To them, fat is a tactile sensation and feels and tastes creamier. Bubbles in fizzy drinks are pricklier. Peppers and other hot foods seem pointlessly painful, like a slap in the face with every bite.

Outside the lab, super-tasters tend to reject bitter things. They find coffee unpleasant and are put off by broccoli, kale and other bitter vegetables. They prefer orange juice to grapefruit. They like cream, cheese and butter. Scientists worry that these people won't get enough cancer-preventing chemicals, since they don't like to eat a wide variety of fruits and vegetables. There's also concern with their penchant for fatty foods. Yet, paradoxically, super-tasters are the thinnest and healthiest of the three groups. Could be that since fat and sugar taste so intense they need less of it to feel sated.

What about the implications for wine tasting? You'd think a super-taster would have the advantage as a connoisseur. Not necessarily. Supers find alcohol, tannins and acids more irritating than tasters and nons do. If they learn to get past the bitterness, though, they can develop very sophisticated palates.

Pregnant super-tasters are especially sensitive to bitter foods, especially in the first trimester when the fetus is most vulnerable. That might explain why 35 percent of women fall into this category, versus only 10 percent of men.

Both overweight and alcoholism correlate with non-tasting. Seems like a pretty dirty trick; not only do you miss out on flavor, you get to be a statistic. What caused this design feature, anyway? Like many atavistic traits it once served an important role.

Back when distinguishing between poisonous and benign fruits was a life or death issue, being a super-taster was a distinct advantage. Non-tasters, in turn, stimulated the rest of the tribe's appetite by going around pointing at everyone's mammoth haunch and saying, "You going to eat that?"

How do you stack up? Here's a simple home test. ("Simple" is used here as a writer's convention. This actually makes a huge mess.) You know those gummy notebook-paper hole-enforcers? Stick one to the front of your tongue. Using a Q-tip, swab blue food coloring over the hole where your tongue is exposed. The blue will sink down, leaving tiny red circles exposed. These are *fungiform papillae*, which contain your taste buds. Count the little guys under a magnifying glass. Forty or more means you're a super-taster. Twenty to forty, you're a taster, and under twenty you're a non-taster. What, you don't have a magnifying glass, Q-tips and blue food coloring handy? Well, don't complain to me about your sex life.

If you turn out to be a super-taster, what do you do, other than embroider an S on your shirt? Try not to reject too many vegetables. Salt helps counteract bitterness (which explains why chocolate, inherently bitter, tastes great over salty pretzels). Stop feeling weird about hating food that other people love. If your kid refuses to eat broccoli or spinach, don't push it; could be he's a super and they taste terrible to him. Look for equally nutritious substitutes he can stand.

As for wine, non-tasters need not despair; most wine appreciation comes through the nose anyway. And now you know: Bad taste is a scientific condition, with no clinical correlation to wearing plaid golf pants.

TALK THE TALK
Finding the words

"A TWINGE OF SOUTH ASIAN MOON FRUIT, laced with blue truffle..." Where do they get this stuff? *You* stick your nose in and smell...um....*wine*. Maybe other things, but...what are they? How do you find the words?

You could just nod knowingly and say, "Well, at this pH level, what do you expect?" No one remembers which pH is which anyway. (Let's see, if the strip turns blue it's acid; pink, it's base. No, wait, blue means base, pink means you're pregnant...)

But wine talk is worth learning. Color, smell, weight, texture, flavors—as verbal creatures we want to name it all, both to communicate the experience and to remember for next time. The right words build a memory bank to judge future wines against.

And they're not just descriptions, they're clues. Words help you home in on subtleties that reveal climate, region and even the people behind a wine.

Wine tasting has a genteel, elegant image, but if you watch the pros they're all snorking, hawking and gurgling, not to mention spitting—in a cup, on the ground, or in a shared spit bucket.

You start by swirling to release aromas. Then, shut your eyes, plunge your nose in and inhale deeply—no dainty sniffs. Pretend you're a bloodhound. They would make great wine tasters if they'd just take notes. (Butt #1: classic, well-aged, mature, developed. Butt #2: full Levis bouquet with a hint of dried Charmin.)

Take a sip and swish it all around. Breathe in through

your mouth to aerate. Breathe out through your nose to acti-vate your retro-nasal route. Spit or swallow, then sigh. Take your time, paying attention to the images and feelings evoked.

You may get that floor polish from kindergarten. Good! Write it down. Something in it is also in this wine. My notes are full of things like, "grandma," "Band-Aid," and "spider webs."

If you're stuck, give your right brain a go: Is the wine sharp or smooth? A high, shrill flute or a rumbling tuba? Dark, stormy night or bright, summer day? We resonate to different metaphors, but starting at opposite ends of *any* spectrum helps narrow your focus.

Another trick is the gimme; in white wines it's apple. You'll find it, but don't stop there. Is it golden delicious? Fuji? Granny Smith, baked, rotten? If there's apple, is there pear? Cherry's the red gimme.

Now you've got a pile of notes crammed with feelings, fruits and improbable things like goat hair. But what good are clues, untranslated?

This is where classes are invaluable. They'll teach you the discipline of a system. If it proceeds from fruit to earth to wood, you won't overlook faint raspberry odor just because smoky oak leads the charge.

But the best part is cracking the code. How cool, to learn that cinnamon, cloves and other Christmas spices say French oak, while coconut and vanilla mean American! Or a certain tongue-drying effect screams Tuscany.

During an introductory course by the Court of Master Sommeliers, I was astounded how quickly newcomers learned to pin down wine. Master Sommelier Doug Frost kept us on course, saying, "First, find three fruits," to a student who had jumped on whiffs of petrol. If we said oak, he'd say, "French or American? Old, soaked barrels or brand new? What percentage new?"

When we placed a wine in the Rhine valley, Frost nudged us to the east bank, saying, "No region but Germany could put in this much flavor at this low alcohol."

Terrified of being called on at first, we were eager by the end of the class to have a go. "Moderate climate, Old World," the guy in front of me began when his turn came. "Wet earth. A Bordeaux blend—mostly Merlot, so…Right Bank. Eight to ten years old." He scoorreesss!! Doug revealed a '95 St. Emilion.

This kind of tasting transcends self-conscious stabs at exotic fruits and flowers. If you're at all interested in wine, I suggest you give it a go. Meanwhile, if you're at a total loss you can always resort to, "I'd call this wine extremely liquid."

GOTCHA!
Unfair, but fun

KING'S RANSOM was the brand of Scotch my great uncle Jascha loved best. He'd pour a little on his hands, rub his palms together and sniff them. "It smells just like perfume," he'd say. This really pissed my father off, because he found the gesture pretentious and the Scotch expensive to keep on hand. Besides, his experiments confirmed that any Scotch, applied this way, smelled like perfume. One day he filled an empty King's Ransom bottle with Black & White and served it to his uncle. Sure enough, after anointing himself, Uncle Jascha pronounced it aromatic as always. This "gotcha" pleased my father immensely.

Wine lovers are probably the number one target of gotchas. They are seen as pompous and elite, and there's nothing quite like knocking them off their pedestal.

In the story "Taste" by Roald Dahl, a stuffy gourmand dines at the house of a friend, who challenges him to name the wine they're drinking, right down to the vintage and vineyard. The host is so sure he's got a ringer that he bets his reluctant daughter's hand in marriage on the outcome. The connoisseur makes an agonizingly slow business of identification, but eventually works his way from grape, to country, to region, to year, to vineyard. And he scores! As the dismayed host prepares to hand over his daughter, the maid appears with a pair of reading glasses belonging to the guest. He had left them, apparently, in the wine cellar. Gotcha!

California is celebrating the 30th anniversary of the gotcha that launched them as players in the international wine scene. In 1976, English wine merchant Steven Spurrier organized a blind-tasting showdown between France and California. Since California was known chiefly for passing off jugs of plonk as "chablis" and "burgundy," France was a shoo-in to win. Imagine the embarrassment of the French judges when they discovered they had placed a Napa Chardonnay first in the white category, beating out a Meursault-Charmes. When it came time for red, much more prestigious, *bien sûr*, they re-doubled their efforts to weed out the Americans. Alas, a '73 Stag's Leap Cab beat Mouton Rothschild. The world took notice and the French have never quite forgiven us.

At least those judges were working. In this mode, they take their tasting pretty seriously. From the first sniff, they search for components that reveal the grape, the climate, the region and the winemaking process. They focus and concentrate. Knowing how seductive a reputation can be, they frequently taste blind, and are often delighted to find the wine they preferred was a $ rather than a $$$. In a social situation, however, they too can relax and drink wine like the rest of us.

Springing a gotcha on someone who's drinking for pleasure is simply cruel. Those who delight in it forget that wine is much more than a liquid. It's tradition, geography and history in a glass. It's a name, a label and memories. It also reflects the context you drink it in. Company, lighting and romance, as well as how many sheets you are to the wind, all affect how wine tastes.

There's no glory in tricking someone by siphoning Coastal Canyon into a Pétrus bottle. Besides, how do you even know your scheme worked? Maybe your mark is just being polite. I certainly never criticize a wine I'm served as a guest. Unless they ask what I think. Which they seldom do again.

Wine should be a pleasure, not a trap. Even puffed-up wine snobs deserve some mercy. And I swear I knew it was Riesling, not Viognier.

Part 6

Bottles & Storage

THIS CATEGORY IS KIND OF A STRETCH, inevitable when you herd a bunch of ornery columns into one corral. The gist is: what you put wine in. It covers bottles with their various corks, screwcaps and other stoppers. Plus cellars, racks, glasses and then, let's not forget, your mouth.

MESSAGE IN A BOTTLE
Shh, it's trying to tell you something

CAN YOU TELL Bordeaux from Burgundy, Chardonnay from Sauvignon Blanc, just by the shape of the bottle? If not, read my crash course on bottle basics. Then impress your friends with this valuable skill.

It begins, as everything does, in history. Wine has been around since before the Neolithic period, but the first wine vessel found dates back to 6000 B.C. Fired pottery had just been invented, and, naturally, the first thing man did was put wine in it. Wine amphorae were sealed with wedges of wood, clay plugs, and often by simply floating olive oil on the surface of the wine, which precipitated the discovery of salad dressing. None of these did a great job of keeping out air, so the resulting oxidized wine was often gussied up with honey, spices, pine resin and things you don't even want to think about.

Glassmaking has been around a long time, but the process

wasn't cheap enough to use for throwaway products like wine bottles until the early 1600s. Even then, they took a while to catch on. Most people preferred life to be a continuous kegger—buying wine in casks and tapping them when they needed a drink. The first bottles were stoppered with rags, wood and occasionally primitive cork pieces, tied securely down around the *string rim*, that lip you often still find at the top of the bottle.

In the early 1800s, the Portuguese perfected the wine cork, which had the effect of gradually changing the shape of the wine bottle. To keep a proper seal, cork must be wet, which means lying bottles on their sides. Roly-poly bottles don't want to lie down and the really round ones don't even allow wine into the neck of the bottle.

In addition, a good seal meant wine could age a lot longer. For the first time, cellars were crammed full of bottles and the most efficient way to do that is stacking them up. Round bottles don't stack well. So bottles began to slim down.

Once bottles were streamlined, you could count on the French to regulate their shapes. We're still using their traditions today. The Bordeaux bottle is a cylinder, because that stacked well for shipping. The bottle's high, square shoulders block the sediment, remnant of years of aging, from pouring into your glass. Dark green glass is for Bordeaux-style reds, such as Cabernet and Merlot and, nowadays, Zinfandel too. Clear glass contains traditional white Bordeaux grapes Sauvignon Blanc and Semillon.

Burgundy bottles have sloping shoulders and a lower center of gravity. Landlocked, Burgundy didn't do much shipping. Its wines are ready younger, and sediment is considered part of the drinking experience. The dark green ones hold Pinot Noir, Syrah (Shiraz) and Beaujolais. Chardonnay goes in a light green Burgundy bottle.

The tall, thin, pointy bottles that never fit in your refrigerator are for Riesling, Gewürztraminer and other Rhine wines.

They can be green, brown or even cobalt blue and faceted. Colored glass is meant to keep out light, with the most age-worthy wines going in the darkest bottles. On the other hand, Sauternes, which can last for centuries, goes in a clear bottle, which just confirms that the French don't always make sense.

There are hundreds of other grapes, of course, and they are free to go in any sort of bottle they wish. Modern wineries, seeking to distinguish themselves in the mass market, come up with weird shapes, such as square on the bottom and round on the top. Some wineries bottle their premium wines in magnums or larger because wine matures more slowly in bigger bottles and can reach a higher level of quality. Now think about this for a moment: A jug holds the same amount as a magnum. Both are perfectly effective glass containers for wine. Yet the magnum is revered while the jug gets no respect. Why? I think it's the name. I mean, "Marilyn's the girl over there with the two big jugs." Might as well say, "While you're at the 7-Eleven, you wanna pick up a couple a hooters of red?"

Heavy bottles are meant to subliminally convey importance and therefore value. The heavy bottle trend is actually getting a little out of hand. Last time I brought wine to a dinner I needed my pack-llama.

Then there's that dent in the bottom of the bottle. What's up with that? Called the punt, or kick, it's absolutely, definitely there for one of the following eight reasons. I just don't know which one.

1. Stability: To keep your Cold Ducks in a row, your base is better off concave than convex.

2. Vestige: The word "punt" derives from *pointu*, a stick that early glassmakers used to anchor the end of the bottle while they blew. When removed, it left a dent.

3. Strength: An important issue for pre-OSHA cellar-rats in Champagne who sometimes wore iron masks to guard against frequently exploding Champagne bottles. ("Poor

Gaston...he just couldn't take the pressure...") Luckily for them, a royal campaign to save the forests forced glassblowers to switch from wood furnaces to coal, resulting in hotter fires and stronger glass. But it was the punched-in bottom that eased pressure and really shored up the design. Check any bottle: You always get a kick with Champagne.

4. **Storage:** Remember the issue of fitting bottles in cellars? Slimmer bottles made a difference, but the kick was instrumental, allowing, as it does, the neck of one bottle to nestle snugly up the ying-yang of the next.

5. **Dregs:** High shoulders may block the dregs, but the trench around the punt traps them before they even get that high.

6. **Deception:** Despite differences in shape, the standard bottle is 750ml, originally one lungful of air for a glassblower. But some bottles manage to look a whole lot bigger than others, while containing the same amount. How do they do that? Why a deeper punt, of course, filling up space inside the bottle.

7. **Pouring:** The precarious and pretentious business, engaged in by some sommeliers, of holding the bottle by its very hind end to pour.

8. **Just Because:** At a restaurant the other day I heard a man explain to his date that a deep dent in the derriere was the sign of a really high quality wine. So the last reason is simply that people think it matters.

Now you know all the secrets. When your host emerges from the cellar bearing bottles you can call out from *way* across the room, "I don't really feel like a Petit Verdot tonight, I'd prefer a Pinot Noir." He will probably whack you over the head which is a proper use for any shape of bottle.

PLAYING TWISTER
The news on screws

"YOUR PRESCRIPTIONS ARE READY, Ms. Rosen. Just wait while I wrap your leeches and fungus in this squirrel pelt."

Absurd? No more so than sealing an expensive, fragile liquid with a chunk of tree bark. Brilliant new technology in 1640, corks could compress to fit in a bottleneck and then expand to keep out air. They ushered in an era of elegant, age-worthy wine and made possible the bottling of another new invention: Champagne. But today, in this age of onboard GPS and solar-powered nose hair clippers, isn't it time for a change?

Consider the problems: Corks only seal when moist. Stand the bottle up and they shrink and let air in. Even lying down, they dry out eventually. That's how the cork crumbles.

They harbor all sorts of wildlife, like the hole-boring cork weevil. Worst critter of all is TCA, the bacteria responsible for "cork taint," often compared to moldy newspapers and vintage gym shorts.

Despite those descriptions, though, most people don't recognize it. They poured corky wine at a James Beard Foundation dinner and no one noticed. I was there accepting an award for a column on—don't laugh—cork taint. So I went around giving the roomful of food luminaries, in many cases, their first comparative whiff.

But even knowing the smell isn't enough, because in smaller concentrations, TCA can rob wine of all vibrant flavors without leaving a trace of its own presence. Winemakers hate this. One corked bottle can turn a customer off their brand for life.

It takes 43 years for a tree to yield high-grade cork. Harvesting is done by hand and axe, followed by six months of curing and then boiling. Sheets of bark are carefully guided by laborers through a punching machine, after which the cork plugs are sorted, dried, sanded, sterilized, bleached, branded, coated, injected with SO_2, bagged and finally shipped.

The recent convergence of young, techno-friendly wine drinkers with a world wine glut that put more bad corks on the market has Portugal, the leading cork producer, scrambling.

They're mounting huge campaigns to prop up their image; cleaning up factories and fighting TCA in ever new ways. When that fails, there are things like Dream Taste, a French invention using ionized copolymers to absorb tainted molecules in wine. The process takes up to an hour, strips other flavors and aromas, and costs $60 plus another $5 for the chemicals to treat each bottle. Plus, you can get the same effect using a Ziploc baggie.

Why bother? Why not switch to…"Screwcaps?" scoff the corkies, "OK for young, frivolous whites. But fine, important reds must breathe oxygen through the cork to age properly." Recent studies, though, show oxygen already present in sufficient amounts. There was a short scare about "reductive," or rotten-egg aromas in wines under screwcap. But they turned out to be winemaking faults, previously covered up by the even worse odor of TCA.

"But, the image, the tradition!" comes the cry. We, the public, they insist, are enamored of pain-in-the-ass cork pulling. Let an appalling percentage of our wine be spoiled, so long as we hear that pop! We might have traded candles for halogen and horses for Pintos, but this, we'll never accept.

Except, apparently, in Australia, now unscrewing some 40 percent of its wine. Or New Zealand, a whopping 90 percent of whose output gets the righty-tighty, lefty-loosy treatment. It seems to be a matter of education. Wine wonks were first to board the screw train. Young trendies who unscrew Tanqueray Ten and Ketel One without complaint are easy converts. "Cork-free zones" are showing up on the wine lists of hipper restaurants.

What of other closures? Bottle caps work, but require a

tool. So do synthetics; besides, they pull away from the bottle neck over time and people think they're ugly. Hybrids are springing up, like Zork, a kind of covered, replaceable, screw/cork thing, and Vino-Lok, an elegant glass stopper secured with rubber O-rings. Both deliver the ever-important pop.

Still, screwcaps lead the pack. "Well then," sputter the cork heads, "how about restaurants? Diners can't possibly enjoy an upscale meal without the pop and circumstance of a good uncorking!"

True, sommeliers are concerned about screwing up the opening ceremony. Do you present the customer with the cap? (The consensus is no; sharp edges are a lawsuit-in-waiting.) I've heard tales of servers covering the cap with a napkin, turning around and making a popping sound with their mouth. Still, all the soms I know are pro-screw.

But, luckily, for those who insist on complicating a simple thing, there's the Wine Fritz: a big metal cap that conceals the small metal cap from sensitive-eyed consumers both during and after the twist-off. It even claims to make a "distinctive sound," although it's more of a grind than a pop.

THE MATRIX PARAMETER
Jell-O shots and nipples

THERE WAS A TIME when wine was drunk from pewter flagons, crockery cups, wooden bowls, and even the bottle itself, which, enclosed in a paper bag, is still de rigueur in certain parts of the world's great capitols. But now we are more sophisticated about getting the most out of wine, and wines have gotten more complex.

If you believe my friend Georg Riedel of Austria, you need a different glass for every drop of wine that hits your tongue. He markets over a hundred different glasses with distinctions so fine that there is one shape for *grand cru* Bordeaux, and another for *mature* Bordeaux. I imagine being pulled over: "Listen, lady, we caught you drinking Pinot Gris from a Pinot Blanc glass. Put your hands in the air and back slowly away from the bottle. Down on the ground! Hands behind your head! I didn't say Simon says! Put your right foot in; put your right foot out. Sorry ma'am, that's what it's all about!"

Back here on earth, though, one or two styles of wine glass suffice for most of us. Given that miserly limitation, what should you look for?

Simplicity, first. Wine glasses should be colorless, even the stem. No cut crystal, no embellishment of any kind. Anything fancy makes it harder to evaluate and enjoy the wine. Those thick, blue, Mexican goblets with bubbles in the glass? They are for margaritas.

The stem and bowl should be thin, and there should be a clean, polished or cut edge on top, not a roll. This allows wine to flow smoothly into your mouth.

The best standard shape is large, ovoid, tapering in at the top. This allows the odors in the wine to concentrate, not evaporate away.

The bowl must be large enough to swirl vigorously without embellishing the wallpaper. Around 10 to 14 ounces for white and 16 to 20 for red works. If you can only have one set, go with about 16 ounces. This is big. But not bigger than your head. That sort of glass brings out the klutz in me. Last time I swirled one, they evacuated New Orleans.

There are hand-blown, lead crystal, $150-a-stem glasses, but I've found very nice ones for as little as $3.50 at outlet stores. Whatever you pay, never fall in love with your wine glasses. They will invariably jilt you in the end. The higher the quality, the quicker you'll break them. Be ready for this.

Here is where I should advise you to wash them in a sink lined with dishtowels, steam over a kettle, air-dry upside down on special racks and…who am I kidding? I put all my crystal in the dishwasher and it looks great. In fact, if I don't, red wine quickly tints it pink. Just don't tell Georg.

So much for today. But what about the future of the wine glass? As an active trend watcher, I'm offering some suggestions. I ask, in return, only credit for my ideas (although I'd consider replacements for the Riedel crystal that my father— given to sweeping, dramatic gestures when he's not grasping at things for balance—keeps breaking).

But that's beside the point because it's time we stopped thinking in dated terms like "wine glass." We've traded in our beds and mattresses for "sleep systems" that do everything from monitoring mood and bone density to charging our cell phone. What we need today is a Beverage Delivery Matrix (BDM).

The BDM concept is important because modern drinking trends are bypassing the glass. Clubbers sip Champagne in cans through bendy straws. Euro-trash disco hounds lick tubes of Freaky Ice frozen pops in flavors like Red Vodka Energy and Tequila & Lime.

Then there's AWOL (Alcohol Without Liquid), a party machine that mixes shots of booze with oxygen to create a vapor you inhale instead of drink. Result: no calories, no hangover, and an instant, euphoric high.

You could fight back with transdermal delivery: a Cabernet cream rubbed on the way athletes take steroids. Or how about a Pinot patch, re-applied every three days, undetectable even to your tailor? It would certainly stem the tide of glass breakage.

For the old or infirm, you might consider a lead-crystal IV bag and tube, or a finely tuned dialysis machine that takes four hours to up the blood's level of the essential Zinfandels.

For the younger set, there's still the Jell-O shot, which showcases varietal flavors while satisfying the urge to chew. No doubt they'll still be at it 50 years hence; a bunch of creaky old snobs at the annual meeting of the Most Honorable Order of Important Wine Worshippers, donning robes, pointy hats and Superman underwear, while out come magnums of vintage Cabernet Jell-O. "Excuse me, sir, but the '02 bounced onto the floor during decanting. Shall I dust it off and serve it anyway?" So obviously the Jell-O shot deserves proper glassware.

What we're all seeking with wine, in the end, is comfort. We've merely replaced mother, lovingly heating our milk bottle in a saucepan, with a sommelier, lovingly chilling our bottle in an ice bucket. With this in mind, your next design project could resemble a baby bottle, with a nipple of softest imported, brushed latex. I don't know, can you hand-blow Pyrex?

The resulting customer satisfaction would more than off-set the R&D costs. This will be big. You'll want to look at acquiring companies such as Evenflo or Gerber. Maybe even Tommee Tippee, whose sippy cup, come to think of it, would make an ideal Christmas present for my dad.

IDIOCY ON THE HIGH SEAS
What's so great about old wine?

AGED IN THE WOOD. Enhanced by time, like a vintage wine. Blah, blah, blah. Wine getting better with age is too useful a metaphor to pry easily out of our brains. It's probably the fault of Orson Welles, droning, "We will sell no wine before its time." The truth is, at most wineries, when the bank calls and says it's time, it's time.

According to recent polls, though, most wine drinkers, including serious geeks, are convinced age is better. When asked to choose between $10 whites that were one, three, or five years old, most opted for the oldest.

They would have been disappointed, had researchers let them try it instead of handing them $5, kicking them out of the lab and chugging it themselves. Lighter whites, the kind in this price range, are quick to lose their fruit and crisp acidity. While the majority of wine hits shelves ready to drink, consumers have this lingering suspicion that if they hold onto it long enough, the antiques show will arrive and hand them millions.

Maybe now that fine wines are coming out in boxes and cans, they should have expiration dates, too, like milk cartons. While they're at it, why not pictures, too? *"**Missing: Clem**. Last seen: Happy Hour. Come home, Clem, your bail bondsman misses you!"*

But there must be something good about age. Consider the lengths people go to for it. Chemical engineer Hiroshi Tanaka, for instance, who spent fifteen years perfecting the Japanese Boffin, a wondrous thing of electrodes, ions and platinum membranes that rearranges atoms to instantly transform rough young plonk into mellow old wine.

Then there's *Retour de l'Inde*. In 1803, Louis-Gaspard d'Estournel, of Bordeaux's Cos d'Estournel, arranged to trade a shipload of wine to a guy in India for a cargo of fine Arabian horses. Packed to her gunnels with barrels of claret, his ship set out on a six-month journey down the coast of Africa, around the Cape of Good Hope, and up through the Indian Ocean. For some reason lost to history, upon the ship's arrival in India, the deal fizzled. Not knowing what else to do, the captain turned around and sailed back to Bordeaux.

When the news and wine got home, D'Estournel figured he'd call the insurance company and stage a Bordeaux Tea Party. But upon tapping a keg, he was astounded to find the wine not only unharmed, but much better than stuff in his own caves from the same vintage. In a flash of marketing genius, he labeled it Retour de l'Inde and doubled the price. Since it was rare, everyone had to have it. It wasn't long before all the fashionable châteaux were sending their wine halfway around the world and back in order to use the trendy term. Retour de l'Inde wine enjoyed a heyday up until 1864 when they built the Suez Canal and spoiled all the fun.

Merely inspired advertising, or was this wine actually better? Crossing the equator four times would subject the wine to enormous temperature variations. The rolling sea would have kept it sloshing around its barrels, exposing more surface area to oxygen. Both processes speed up aging. In those days, without the technology to make fruity, easy-drinking wine, most was pretty harsh and needed years in the cellar to be palatable.

When wine ages, oak and aroma compounds bond to produce hundreds of fragrant, new molecules. Malic acid, the stuff that discolors sliced apples, causes white wine to darken to gold or brown. Reds go from purple to red/brown to orange, and harsh tannins soften, as their pigments bond together and sink to the bottom of the bottle. Along with dead yeast cells and other gunk, they become sediment—the reason you shouldn't shake up an old bottle before pouring.

Aging turns fresh fruit into a complex, nutty essence known as bottle bouquet. If you've been raised on New World fruit bombs, get ready to recalibrate your palate. The taste of age can be disappointingly subtle, a little like tuning into a string quartet on your way home from a rock concert. Or, as California's seminal winemaker André Tchelistcheff put it: "Appreciating old wine is like making love to a very old lady. It is possible. It can even be enjoyable. But it requires a bit of imagination."

There's also the problem of finding an older bottle. If you do, there's no guarantee it hasn't been sleeping all those years over heat ducts, becoming vintage vinegar.

If your children have reached an age where it seems sane to leave them something, you might consider laying down your own bottles. Assuming your cellar is cool, dark and quiet, what should you look for? Standard keepers include reds from Bordeaux and Rioja, whites from Alsace and Burgundy and dessert stickies like French Sauternes and German

Trockenbeerenauslese. But that's just a start. Age-worthy wines come from all over the globe. Good candidates need a foundation of preservatives, i.e., acid, tannin, and/or sugar, along with exuberant fruit and something else—that indescribable extra that makes them exciting enough to want to revisit. You can probably rule out anything with an animal on the label.

Slower aging means a more intricate bouquet. Both over-sized bottles and screwcaps help, by limiting oxygen contact (although dyed-in-the-cru corkies still insist on a piece of tree-bark crammed down the neck of the bottle).

How long should you wait before drinking? Ah, my child—how deep is a hole? How high is up? Alas, like in the stock market, you only know the perfect moment when it's gone. Best to approach it like a kid opening Christmas presents: So what if one's a sweater from grandma—the next might be a pony! Avoid total tragedy by buying at least six bottles and cracking one open every few years to check; if you drink no wine before its time, you'll drink some pretty sorry wine. On the other hand, at least you don't have to write a thank you note to grandma for it.

If all this seems way complicated, you could try loading a case in the trunk and driving to Tijuana and back. But don't ask Mr. Tanaka. He only uses his Boffin on coffee and cheap whiskey. Doesn't much like wine, himself.

CAVING IN
To store and protect

THE FACT THAT great-aunt Laura didn't drink never stopped friends from bringing the occasional bottle of wine as a house present. I found this out as a delinquent child and frequent visitor, when I discovered the key to her liquor closet. Knowing something about wine from my parents, who *did* drink, my idea of fun was squatting in front of her cramped liquor cabinet and lying all the wine bottles down on their sides. Summer temperatures, hovering in the nineties, doomed these bottles anyway, still, I wanted to give them a sporting chance. Every week, the housekeeper would return them to their full and upright positions. Try as I might, I could not convince either lady my way was better. When Aunt Laura died, they found an underground room full of prohibition-era liquor, some of it homemade. In addition, some old and priceless Bordeaux. All standing up. All ruined.

Wipe the tear from your eye now and we'll learn from her mistakes. If you're not enough of a wine wonk to own your own storage unit or cellar, these five rules should keep your wine collection from becoming another tragic statistic.

1. Position. Oxygen is the enemy. Corks only seal it out when they are swollen with liquid. If you let them dry, they shrivel like an old balloon. To keep the cork wet, always store bottles on their side, with the neck pointing slightly down. Commercial wine racks usually do this, but if you make your own, boost the butt of the bottle to be sure. As the trend towards screwcaps gains steam I envision the day when all bottles can stand up proudly. And wine racks will be designed quite differently.

2. Temperature. When they talk about serving wine at room temperature, they're referring to a room in a 500-year-old, damp, stalactite-ridden château. Around 55° Fahrenheit, to be exact. Wine stored at 75° will age twice as fast. Consistency matters, though, so a steady 60° is better than a room with wild temperature swings.

3. Light. Another enemy. You know those wrought-iron, grape-leaf garland wine racks, or the gee-whiz, cantilevered bottle holders you're supposed to keep on display? Sorry. If you have one, put out a bottle or two you're going to drink this week, but the rest should go somewhere dark and out of sight.

4. Humidity. 60 percent is ideal, though where I live in Colorado you won't find it outside the Bronco's locker room.

Another reason it's crucial to keep those corks wet from within; our weather is doing its best to dry them from without.

5. Vibration. There are no good vibrations with wine. Next to the washing machine won't do. Don't practice your pogo stick or your jackhammer nearby either.

If you can't remember all this, just think: if Dracula would be happy there, so will your wine. Since 90 percent of wine is bought to drink right away, you might think none of this matters, but all you have to do is get a couple of bottles ahead of your drinking and suddenly storage is an issue.

As for opened wine, if you can't down 750ml in one sitting, store it, corked, in the fridge. Air is the enemy here, and it sits in the space between what's left in the bottle and the cork. That space is known as *ullage*, as in, "Ullage you have the rest of this bottle if you'll shut up and go away." You can foil ullage by saving some smaller bottles and funneling your leftovers into them. Another fix is topping the bottle up, as winemakers do with barrels. Just fill it to the top with a similar wine. Mixing wine isn't against the law.

Table wines are usually OK for a day or two. Fortified, sweet and very alcoholic wines can last a whole lot longer. Some very young, very tannic wines will actually be better the next day or two. And sparkling wine stays fresh for days with no stopper, needing only the cold temperature to hang onto its bubbles.

Perhaps I'd never have learned all this without the traumatic bottle abuse I witnessed as a child. But the Aunt Laura story had a happy ending. While the wine was ruined, we found some carboys of bathtub gin that weren't half bad. They certainly perked up the funeral.

TO HAVE & TO HOARD
Dissecting collectors

IF YOU LOVE WINE, people assume you collect it. I don't happen to collect anything, myself, but studies say fully one third of us do, be it Hummel figurines, Coke memorabilia or Picassos. What was once a hobby for merchants and kings is common sport now that today's trash is quickly tomorrow's collectible and fortunes are won and lost on eBay.

The urge to collect appears to be hard-wired. Like other biological imperatives—eating and sex come to mind—sometimes it goes haywire. It's a small step from a cellar of premier cru to a house full of cats and old *National Geographics*.

No doubt the hoarding instinct developed to store food, but your average collectible isn't much use for surviving a long winter. It has a different sort of value, in many cases nothing more than the glow implied by where it's been. A bottle of Thomas Jefferson's (now undrinkable) Madeira! A ball hit out of the field by Bubbie Schwartz! A diaper soiled by Elvis! All magic totems, believed to bestow power on the lucky owner.

The bottles I keep on hand for guest ambushes and my state's blue-law Sundays not only lack provenance, but, like the CDs scattered around my house and car, they lack another crucial feature of collections: theme. Sorting and organizing is an integral part of the true collecting compulsion. No one lusts for three widgets or eight, but the *whole set*. Which must then be catalogued, compared and displayed.

My bottles are neither expensive nor rare, requirements if you're collecting for social status. A case or two of cult wines—bottlings allocated to a tiny, exclusive list—certifies you as clever, well-connected or simply rich enough to play with the big boys. That sort of collecting is no fun without an audience, a requirement for the classic wine-bore. You know, the type who shows you all around his precious cellar and then offers you a glass of Beaujolais Nouveau.

I say "his," because while women may collect stuffed animals and Depression glass, wine collecting is mainly a man's world. America's top two wine auctioneers were unable to name me even one great female collector.

Of course, they preside over a fairly male phase of collecting: the hunt. But the once-exclusive auction world has recently been invaded by riff raff who cut their teeth on e-bidding. A great surge in faxed and e-mailed bids is not only moving things down-market, but changing the essential auction dynamics. The frenzy that infects a mob and sends bids through the roof, that rhythmic tide of excitement as each lot builds to climax—all that fizzles with remote bidding.

The tradition lives on, however, at the charity wine auction, an invitation-only proving ground for the nascent big shot. The game here is conspicuous overspending, to show the world you've arrived.

My bottles pile up out of equal parts love and neglect, but some people collect purely for investment. Wine makes a cruel hedge fund. At least with a painting you can fill the space above the couch and admire brushwork while you wait for it to appreciate into something your children will fight over when you're dead. Alas, you can't have your Cab and drink it too. No sooner enjoyed but worthless, sometimes it's even rude enough to expire before you even open it.

But many collectors don't care—they're not planning on drinking it.

Some simply amass too much for a lifetime. One collector I know has a whole cellar wing set aside for his funeral. It's mostly dessert wine, which he doesn't even like, but he bought because it was important. I, on the other hand, adore sweet wine, and shall consider it an honor to toast his memory some day with '67 Yquem.

Unlike so many, though, he actively enjoys his collection.

He plays in the cellar with the sensual bliss of King Midas in gold, hefting bottles, admiring and rearranging them. He buys them humidifiers and neck tags the way a little girl accessorizes her Barbie or a Hell's Angel his Harley. He's also not averse to opening the good stuff for guests. In short, my kind of collector.

Part 7

Labels

WHY DO LABELS get a whole section of their own? Because most people a) choose wine based on them, and b) have no idea how to read them. But you're not most people. By the end of this section you'll be speaking fluent Labelese. I hear the government is looking for translators.

A LITTLE KNOWLEDGE
Buying by the label

"THE OTHER DAY," writes a friend, "my 11-year-old daughter insisted I buy a bottle of wine that had a picture of a jumping horse on it—Leaping Pony or something. For a kid with no interest in wine but much interest in sailing over fences on a pony, the label and name were enough. It cost all of $4.99 and was actually not bad. But you probably already know the creative techniques used by many morons in this country to select their wines...."

If choosing products by label is for morons, count me among them. Wine is for pleasure, and part of that pleasure is the delicious fantasies that brands inspire. How do you buy shampoo? Do you visit the Pantene factory? Study *Consumer Reports*? I doubt it. Most of us simply let ourselves be seduced by a label promising shiny, manageable tresses.

Suppose you bought a car purely so it would catapult you into a world of infinity-edged pools, where women wear up-do's, hubcaps never get grimy and concierges know you by name? That would be fairly moronic. But when stakes are low, who cares? How bad can it be if your comb over refuses to become a lion's mane or a wine doesn't live up to its promise?

Readers confess all the time to the sin of label shopping—always with the guilty implication that obviously *smart* people know better. We consult lawyers, shipbuilders and psychics. We proudly proclaim our inability to program our VCR, when by now most of us really do know how. Yet we think we're supposed to be wine experts, or, short of that, have no opinion.

When people learn I write about wine, they get nervous and apologetic, saying things like, "Oh, I don't know anything about wine—I just drink beer and, uh, let other people choose the wine. Yeah, that's the ticket." Like I'm about to pop a quiz they didn't get around to studying for.

I suppose I could be a little insulted. They think with a few minute's effort they should have mastered my career as well as their own. When you find out someone's a brain surgeon, you don't generally say, "Oh, I don't know anything about brain surgery; when I get a tumor I just grab a screw driver and kind of wiggle it around in my ear…"

Just as we suspect other people of having more and better sex, of never bouncing checks or eating between meals or peeing in the bathtub like we do, we credit them with knowing more than us about wine. People from the right families learn to tell Bordeaux from Burgundy in the crib, right? For all the help your parents were, you might as well have been raised by wolves.

Michael Apstein, wine writer for the *Boston Globe*, notes, "You ask people what they think about a movie and you get a longwinded answer. You ask people what they think about a restaurant and you get a longwinded answer. You ask people to comment about wine and you get the deer in the headlamps."

When ordering dinner, you may factor in carb count or peanut allergies, but seldom the waiter's opinion. The wine list is something else: It's as though we're convinced Allen Funt secretly planted a Stupid Wine and if we choose it bells will ring, our pants will fall down and we'll drop into a dunk tank. True, the pressure with food is not quite so unnerving. The waiter doesn't hover as you cut, chew and swallow the first bite, waiting for your nod confirming that the butter is indeed creamery, the sausage: country, and the eggs: farm-fresh.

But perhaps you just happen to have a life. Australian marketing specialist Dr. Larry Lockshin divides wine drinkers into two categories: High-Involvement and Low-Involvement. HIs read wine magazines and discuss appellations. They spend big bucks, but are also alert to sales and bargains from new regions. LIs just want to drink the stuff. They stay with familiar brands and price ranges and don't give a damn about wine-maker philosophy or vintage reports.

My weekly wine column runs in a daily paper, not a wine magazine, so I assume it reaches far more LIs than HIs. Certainly requests for a good $6.99 wine far outnumber those for reports on the Bordeaux futures market. More than one reader has confessed to, a) knowing nothing about wine, and b) reading my column every week, for years. I like to think this reflects more on their involvement level than on my teaching prowess.

It's OK not to make the study of wine one of life's big priorities. Besides, even geeks like me shop by label sometimes. It's fun!

If I pick the right one, there's always the chance I'll find myself sipping it under a *palapa* while chiseled pool boys feed me caviar and massage my feet. Might as well savor the whole package, from the picture outside to the wine within.

ANIMAL FARM
Wine is going to the dogs...and monkeys...and kangaroos

MY CELLAR IS TURNING INTO A ZOO: Yellow Tail, Smoking Loon, Busted Buzzard, Spanking Monkey. One night I hear this noise in the cellar and I go down to find nothing left but some shards of glass and a big bottle of Drooling Lion. I'm thinking about hiring that Australian guy to keep them in line: "Steady there little guy, I'm just getting your cork out. Crikey! I think he bit me!"

Front line in the battle for consumer's wallets, the wine label gets weirder and weirder. It remains the deciding factor in most wine sales, despite the best efforts of wine writers who bust their butts to educate. To be noticed amidst today's increasing flood of good wine, labels have to practically wave their arms and shout, "Hey! Over here! Look at me!"

Spidery Old World penmanship is out. Aristocratic crests and gold lettering that once guaranteed respectability now scream, "Stuffy!" Apparently consumers are sick of respecting wine—they want to have fun with it, tease it, pull its hair. The message these days is: we ain't your father's Bordeaux.

Even Bordeaux is saying it. Check out, in a screwcap if you please, Soyons Simple. The translation, Let's Be Simple isn't quite as catchy, but you get the point. There's no mystery about the big red truck on France's Van Rouge. Stateside, the Gnekow Family Winery pares it down to basics with a bottle labeled simply: YN.

Self-conscious simplicity, though, like English wine Great with Chicken, risks spilling into cutesiness. Or worse: folksy treacle like Ideal with Friends, which sports playschool drawings and the syrupy slogan, "A wine to share."

The dumbing-down trend partly explains the attack of the critter wines, but mostly they're just following the leader, in this case, Australian phenom Yellow Tail. This not particularly good wine rose bafflingly from nowhere with no advertising to over five million cases in 2004, becoming the top selling red in America and capturing 30 percent of the Aussie market share, close to giants Southcorp and Rosemount combined.

The little kangaroo hopped from the label stable of Australian designer Barbara Harkness, who calls her ready-to-wear brand service "Just Add Wine." U.S. importer Bill Deutsch was skeptical at first. "Having a kangaroo on the front label is like having an Eiffel tower on a French wine," he scoffed.

No one can explain the brand's wild success, but, according to the Global Color Survey, it could be the bright yellow label, which signals "Happy." Making it a better choice than, for instance, red, which consumers associate with "Stop!" and "Danger."

Yet it's not the color, but the don't-worry, be-hoppy marsupial that's spawned a menagerie of copy cats. There's Hair of the Dingo, with its whimsical little dog and a name that telegraphs both its origin and when to drink it. Cat's Pee on a Gooseberry Bush, seems like an odd name for New Zealand Sauvignon Blanc unless you know it's a common way of describing the smell of this grape. Fairview's Goats do Roam and Goat Rôtie from South Africa stick it to the French and their stuffy old (Côte du Rhône and Côte Rôtie) appellations.

Spatzendreck, from South Africa's Delheim winery, is winemaker Spatz Sperling's nose-thumb to critics. Spatz means sparrow; the label shows one cheerfully lifting his tail and depositing a drop of, well, dreck, into the bunghole of a barrel.

The slathering tiger on Bonny Doon's Bloody Good White has just polished off a wine critic, to judge from the hastily abandoned tasting notes. Deep in the woods, the plush Bearitage mascot squeezes a grape cluster into his mouth.

But there's more than animals in the jungle. On Alexander Valley's Sin Zin label, a languid fellow in hose and jerkin reclines on the forest floor, drinking wine from a horn. A lady pouring for him on the original edition was judged entirely too naked for the American market.

She follows a censoring tradition reaching back to the first toga parties etched on amphorae. Mouton Rothschild's 1993 artist label—a sketch of a naked girl by Balthus—was banned in America. They should have known. Back in 1975, Kenwood's first Artists Series label, another reclining nude (don't women ever stand or squat?) was deemed too racy for our sensibilities. A bit petulant, Kenwood removed her flesh and submitted a reclining skeleton, which was also rejected. Then, in 1995, the ATTTB suddenly relented on the original picture, breasts and all, which is bizarre considering the bare chested Queen of Clubs on Australian producer Peter Lehmann's bottle was told to leave her nipples at the border. The original artist was obliging enough to paint in a few more inches of shirt. I don't know about you, but I certainly feel safer knowing our Titty Tsar is on the job, rounding up and bra-ing outlaw mammaries.

Wiser labels just suggest. The Full Montepulciano, from Abruzzo, Italy, shows only a narrow tie snaking through the air, flung by someone just outside the picture. And no one suggests like Norma Jean. The estate-licensed Marilyn Merlot sells out quickly at any price, sometimes to people who don't even like the wine. They can't help it, they say, they love her.

Other charismatic corpses, too, are hard at work flogging vintages. Elvis is rocking the vine with Jailhouse Red Merlot, The King Cabernet Sauvignon and Blue Suede Chardonnay. Meanwhile, a CBS News producer filed an application for the name "Jesus Juice," coined by Michael Jackson for kiddy-plying purposes. A barely-clad, crucified figure graces the label, complete with a sequined glove, shiny loafers, stringy hair, and a black fedora obscuring his face.

Hitler's no slouch, either, nor is Mussolini. Both appear on an Italian label proclaiming "One People, One Empire, One Leader." Rommel, Goering, Stalin and Marx are just a few of the other charmers who have graced producer Lunardelli's bottles.

Bad taste sells, as Russian River's Stu Pedasso could tell you. Witness California's White Trash White and Redneck Red, featuring portraits of trailer park royalty and the slogan "No catfish should be served without it." Old Tart, England's contribution to crass, features a shopworn floozy and the advice "Be smart, enjoy the tart." Her brother-in-smarms, the similarly depraved Old Git, was re-dubbed Old Fart for our side of the pond. Probably the most famous gross-out wine is Fat Bastard, whose sales soared when Mike Meyers climbed into a giant rubber bodysuit.

Then there's Australia's Rude Boy and Rude Girl. Put the bottle in the fridge, and they lose their respective shorts and dress. The thermo gimmick is popular. The fish on Australia's White Point bottle swim serenely until chilled down; then the great white shark attacks. More practically, the thermometer on Loire valley's Ten Degrees changes color at the ideal serving temperature.

For even more action, check out the hologram on Argentine Bodega Norton's Lo Tengo. Rotate the bottle, or just walk around to see a dancing couple dip and swerve.

Interactive labels are another way to draw in customers. England's Saintsbury Market wines come with a recipe that peels off, so guests will think the truffled weasel snouts pairing was your idea. Blind tasters can cheat with Michel Chapoutier's Braille labels, while keeping their social responsibility intact.

If all this is too much for you, you could reach for a wine from France in a red bottle, with a red label and red cork that calls itself "Red." The wine inside? Chardonnay. Apparently life is not always simple. One Hungarian winery faces this fact squarely, calling its wine "The Unpronounceable Grape." That grape, for the record, is Cserszegi Fuszeres, and I could tell you how to pronounce it but then they'd have to change the label. And kill you.

GIRLS JUST WANNA HAVE…WHA-UH?
Marketing to women

THE FOLLOWING URGENT STORY punctuated my normal flow of press releases that announce, at least a dozen times a day, that such and such a winery has just….*released a wine!* What WILL they think of next?

Wineries, apparently, have been forced by competition to wake up and smell the marketing, a nasty business on which Anheuser-Busch alone spends ten times as much as the entire wine industry.

While examining who their customers were, producers discovered who they weren't: most of the country. In fact, 13 percent of people drink 89 percent of the wine, and 43 percent never lift a glass at all. This, the industry concluded, reflected fear, thus setting off a stampede towards stupidity. Wine Guides for Dummies, Morons, Cretins and Nit-wits multiplied and a menagerie of Grazing Bunnies, Drunken Anteaters and Busted Buzzards migrated across labels, as everyone tried to be the next Stock-Splitting Kangaroo.

When the zoo overflowed, producers turned to serious, demographic market segmentation, where they discovered, as if from out of the depths of a mummy's tomb, a hitherto unknown group: women! Yes, indeed, despite the stereotype of magnum-measuring males, it turns out 77 percent of wine is bought by women, who then turn around and drink 60 percent of it. And we're not just talking supermarket; babes buy 60 percent of high-end bottles, too. How to stalk this intriguing new species? A hundred focus groups, book clubs and Internet surveys later, came the astounding conclusion that women are (well, rip my pantyhose!) emotional. They drink wine as a casual beverage with—get this—friends! They're also busy, and they find wine helps them transition from work day to play night.

Woman-as-target always struck me a bit, as it were, broad.

In my experience, women's skis don't bash bumps better; jeans cut for a woman's curves don't hug mine, and what's up with genders for perfume and deodorant? It's not like women exude sugar and spice while men sweat.

Nevertheless, the race is on to serve Woman. Whoever that is. Because wineries define her quite differently. For example:

Mom. An edgy frau with psychotic smile brandishes an eggbeater on the label of Mad Housewife Chardonnay and Cabernet Sauvignon, while back copy references plastic yard toys, litter boxes and "the cool shadows of the laundry room." Store displays include 1950s-style refrigerators, cleaning supplies and processed foods.

Temptress. Seduction, a "voluptuous, fleshy fusion with sensual flavors and velvet kiss," is wrapped in a translucent organza garment, ready to be ripped, bodice-like, from its heaving...punt? In a bid to be "approachable," the label omits such technical mumbo jumbo as, say, grape varieties, but then swooning females don't need facts.

Ingenue. Fontana Candida is courting the novice, repositioning itself as the "fun, fashionable and tasteful accessory to young women's personal sense of style and sophistication." Bottles are adorned with colorful slips and feathers, presumably so the resourceful *Glamour-Cosmo* girl can drink the wine and then turn the whole thing into a darling purse.

Air-Head. White Lie Early Season Chardonnay, both local and lo-cohol, is achieved by picking grapes before sugar rises too high, then de-alcoholizing further down to 9.8 percent. The bait is set with girly-curly lettering on a lipstick-red label and corks are inscribed with yeah-right lines like, "I'll be home by seven," and "It's my natural color."

Redneck Gal. Look for the union label when buying Working Girl White, Go Girl Red and Rosé the Riveter. Ad copy nails the full repertoire of sisterhood: "Everyday wines for everyday friends," "A salute to working women everywhere,"

"Created by women for women in support of women" and "No sophisticated research...just three working women who have raised families, held full-time jobs and kept households running." Clichés of the world, unite.

Lest a feminine heartstring be left un-tugged, many of the new crop of she-wines make a big deal of supporting various medical causes involving gyno-plumbing, a goodly thing that nevertheless does little to whet my appetite and much to set off my manipulation meter. At the risk of sounding insensitive: Gag me with a corkscrew.

When the day comes for a true woman's wine, Ben and Jerry will make it. I have no idealistic beef against marketing. Actually, I love it. So why does this trend irritate me so? Putting aside personal, tomboy distaste, I find wines designed by focus group tend towards lowest common denominator blandness. They lose all relation to the living, ever-changing, mystery-in-a-bottle, and then wine ceases to be the most interesting of all drinks and becomes just another product. I'm sorry, but it makes me sad. That may be irrational, but what do you expect from a woman?

YOU SAY MERITAGE
And you probably say it wrong

MERITAGE IS ONE OF THOSE WORDS that's often misunderstood and mispronounced. While the proper pronunciation of valet (valette or vallay?) and chaise longue (long or lounge?) come down to whether you want to come off as a French or a British snob, Meritage is a registered trademark with an official pronunciation.

And an official meaning, which I learned the hard and humiliating way. After describing it in a column as something to

117

the effect of "a whole bunch of grapes all smooshed up together," I was sternly scolded by a member of the Meritage association who put me straight. So I'm going to assuage my chagrin by doing the same with you.

The whole wine-naming business is complex enough to discourage many consumers. The concept to remember is that some countries name wine after a place, and some after a grape. France, (whose Ministry of Lined-Paper mandates that I use a legal pad and fountain pen for 35.2 percent of my writing) tightly regulates what can be grown, where. The only red grapes allowed in Burgundy, for example, are Pinot Noir and Gamay, while whites are all Chardonnay. (Little-known fact: the guillotine was invented in 1726 to dispense with parsley farmer Giles LeMoof of Givry, Burgundy, who mistakenly grafted a piece of chervil onto what turned out to be Sauvignon Blanc rootstock.)

America simplified matters by putting everything in jugs and calling it chablis or burgundy. Or in the same jug and called it rosé. These wines bore no relation to *real* Chablis and Burgundy, a mistake that scared at least half the population away from ever drinking wine again.

To disassociate themselves from these generics, serious winemakers introduced the *varietal*, a wine named after its grape. Wine labeled Petite Sirah, for instance, must contain at least 75 percent Petite Sirah. So, we began buying wines called Syrah and Merlot instead of Côte-Rôtie and Bordeaux.

Varietals are great, but there's a reason the French blend. Nature is unpredictable. If your Cabernet is pale this year, you can punch up the color by adding Petit Verdot. If it's harsh or tannic, Merlot will help soften it.

In America, blends must be labeled Table Wine, which is kind of the vinous equivalent of Spam. Besides, with so many fantasy names for blends, like *Symphony*, *Tapestry* and *Trilogy*, consumers were confused. So, in 1988, the Meritage Association was born. To qualify for the designation, a wine must contain two or more of the traditional Bordeaux grapes, with no one grape making up more than 90 percent of the blend. The red grapes allowed are Cabernet Sauvignon, Cabernet Franc, Merlot, and five others that will not be on the test. The five white grapes include Sauvignon Blanc and Semillon. A Meritage may not contain, for instance, Chardonnay or Zinfandel, since neither is a Bordeaux grape. The idea is for the word Meritage to conjure up the same associations as the word Bordeaux, namely, a specific style of wine, excellent quality, and a defibrillator once you've seen the price. Only kidding. CPR works just as well.

The name combines *merit* and *heritage*, and rhymes with the latter. However, since people pretend to speak French when they find themselves out of their depth, you'll often hear Meri*tahge*, as in Mahal. That is wrong.

I am therefore deputizing you, as patriotic Americans, to go forth and correct people. When you hear someone refer to Meri*tahge*, you can confidently interrupt them to explain what an idiot they are, in as loud a voice as possible. It worked on me.

CRACKING THE CODE
Be a label sleuth

STUCK IN A WINE RUT, but don't know where to turn? If you're ready to branch out and try something new, but wary of wasting good folding money on wine fit for the garbage disposal, it pays to become a label detective. The label is a treasure-trove of clues to finding that hidden gem you're scouting for.

So grab your bottle, find a magnifying glass (you'll need it to find the alcohol percent) and let's get started.

1. Producer

Obvious if it says "Joe's Winery." But some producers hide like they were Waldo, putting a *proprietary name* (see #2) up front.

Example:
<small>Banfi</small> C E N T I N E

Some wineries have second labels—often great wine at a lower price. French seconds use words like "cadet" (little brother) or derivatives of the main name.
Examples:
"Mouton Cadet," "Fleur de Pétrus."

2. Proprietary Name
A made-up name for a special blend or a wine that doesn't contain enough of one grape to list it on the label.
Examples:
Flora Springs' "Trilogy," Hugel's "Cuvée Les Amours."

3. Grape
The percentage of a grape required to list it on the bottle varies from 100 percent in Alsace down to 75 percent in Sonoma. The grape can be tricky to find on Italian labels, since it's often part of the appellation, and with hundreds of indigenous grapes, chances are you've never heard of it, anyway. It doesn't show up on French labels at all, except on Vin de Pays and in Alsace.

4. Appellation
Appellations are layered over one another. America is one; each state is also one; within each state are regional appellations like Central Coast and Napa Valley, and within those are even smaller appellations, some as tiny as a single vineyard.

Which appellation does a winemaker use? The smallest. The more specific the appellation, the more prestigious, expensive, and generally, better, the wine.

In the New World, appellations are simply geographical regions where the grapes are grown.

In Europe, appellations also include regulations about grape variety, tonnage, irrigation, sugar level at harvest, resulting wine style and winemaker's eye color.

5. Year

The year the grapes were *harvested*. It's important to know about a particular vintage if a) you're buying expensive wine, b) you're planning to age it, or c) it comes from a region with unreliable weather. As vineyard science and winemaking develop, though, vintages are becoming less important. They scarcely differ at all in Australia.

6. Quality Classification

A European thing. The EU classification system separates ordinary table wine from higher qualities. Within the EU levels, each country has its own system of conferring sanctity on certain producers and vineyards, often varying by region. Legally, these are so hard to change that some wineries rest on laurels granted 150 years ago. Some hardly deserve them anymore while others show amazing consistency.

Examples:

France:
~ AOC (Appellation d'origine controllée),
    Grand Cru Classé

Italy:
~ DOC (Denominazione d'origine controllata),
    DOCG, IGT

Spain:
~ DO (Vinos de Denominación de Origen), DOCa

Germany:
~ QmP (Qualitätswein mit Prädikat), QbA.

121

7. Style Statement

Tells whether it's dry, sparkling or dessert wine.

Examples:

Vendange Tardive, Sélection de Grains Nobles, Trockenbeerenauslese, or anything else implying late harvest or special selection of individual grapes, means sweet wine.

Moussant, spumante, frizzante all denote sparklers and sound like it but so does *sekt* which doesn't.

Trocken means dry. Most dry wines don't say anything.

8. Quality Statement

"Vintner's Special Private Reserve Cellar Selection, etc." In the New World, these have no legal meaning at all. Some wineries save Reserve for their best bottlings, some for wines they've tarted-up with oak, while still others slap it on their cheapest junk. Hence "Reserves" at $6, which kind of makes hash of the whole concept.

In the Old World, however, many of these words are legal statements that vary by country and region.

Examples:

Spain:

~ *Reserva* = aged three years; one in barrel and two in bottle.

~ *Gran Reserva* = aged five years; two in barrel and three in bottle.

Italy:

~ *Riserva* = only for DOC or better wines, higher alcohol level, aged at least three years, with more specific regional requirements.

9. Bottling Statement

Produced, Bottled and Vinted by Joe. In general, the more

involved the winemaker is in each step, the better. "Estate Bottled" means the same folks grew (or at least contracted) the grapes, and made and bottled the wine on the property. At the other extreme, "Cellared by Joe," or "Vinted and Bottled by Joe," means that God-knows-who made the wine and Joe just slapped on his label.

10. Alcohol Percentage

Worth checking. You can knock back a lot of German Riesling kabinett at 8 percent and be little the worse for it, while the same amount of California Zinfandel at 16.5 percent leaves you face-down in your tapas. Alcohol adds body, viscosity, sweetness and aromas, so high-alcohol wines are an all-around more intense experience.

11. Back Label

Info on malolactic fermentation and steel tanks versus oak barrels clues you in on style. Beware references to "oak" without the word "barrel," as in "nuances of toasty French oak." Barrels cost a bundle. Some wineries save by just tossing in chips or extract for oak flavor. True barrel aging may add no oak flavor at all. But it concentrates wine through evaporation, adds richness to texture and helps with graceful aging.

Sometimes there will be a folksy story about Scooter, the faithful barn cat, who discovered the vineyard and likes to sleep in the Carmenère. Big marketing departments hire people like me to come up with this stuff.

Tasting notes, like: "A crisp wine, with gobs of Asian moon fruit on the mid-palate and a swoosh of pungent finnberry on the long finish…" are generally one part winemaker's ego to two parts copywriter's fantasy. Any resemblance to wine inside, living or dead, is purely coincidental.

Those Crazy Italians!

ITALIAN APPELLATIONS CAN CONSIST OF:

Place only:
- ~ **Barolo**
- ~ **Chianti**

Grape and **place**:
- ~ *Barbera* **d'Asti**
- ~ *Verdicchio* **di Castelli di Jesi**
- ~ *Sangiovese* **di Romagna**

Place and *grape*:
- ~ **Colli di Scandiano** *Sauvignon*

Place and TYPE or STYLE:
- ~ **Montello** ROSSO
- ~ **Asti** SPUMANTE

OLD WORLD / NEW WORLD LABEL DIFFERENCES	
Old World (Europe)	New World (Rest of PLANET)
Blended grapes "Chardonnay," etc.)	Varietals ("Merlot,"
Appellation = region plus growing, production and style requirements	Appellation = growing region
Place more important	Grape more important
Quality classifications	"Reserve" free-for-all

Part 8

Choosing & Ordering

YOU'VE MADE IT THIS FAR. You vaguely remember one or two points from the first seven sections. Now it's show time. You've got to put all the info together and choose a wine! There's always the risk of choosing wrong. You might choose wrong. Don't worry, they'll only laugh at you for a few weeks.

RECCING MACHINE
How and why I recommend the wines I do —

WHILE YOU DEVOTE YOUR LIFE to something useful, I spend my days pouring and swirling, sloshing and uncorking, to find wines worthy of recommending. It sounds like I drink a lot of wine, but actually I spit most of it. Otherwise, Ripple and Thunderbird would make the third-round cut.

For every star I find, I taste around 20 baddies. Another 10 percent are corked, phenolic, or otherwise ruined, so I don't know what I might have missed.

Sometimes I request a specific wine for a story, but more often is just shows up, like manna from heaven—if you had to chew manna, spit it out and write about it—from wineries, PR firms and importers. All day long. I answer the doorbell in bathrobe, towel, evening dress, cowboy outfit. The neighbors think I run a novelty cathouse for delivery drivers.

I shoot for a mix of price ranges and availability. At any given moment, a particular wine might be carried only at retail, only in restaurants, in both, in neither, or simply be sold out. Some wines get lauded so fast and universally that by the time the ink dries on reviews you can't find them. Just try buying anything in the annual top ten from *Wine Spectator*. Once in a while I lob in something rare and wonderful like, for instance, Hungarian Tokaj, which I don't expect to show up at Sam's Lube 'n Luberon.

Movie critics have it easy. Their screening rooms reek of the same old popcorn and chewing gum. They don't have to combat the objectivity factor: being wined, dined and romanced.

For most purposes, wine just isn't very objective stuff. We all fall in love with labels, ideas and memories. For example, how could you forget that evening in Phraxistan, dining on sloth gizzards—a local delicacy—in that cliff-side café at sunset, while gondoliers frolicked below with dolphins in the surf? From somewhere nearby floated the soft sounds of a peasant strumming his blourqua. You glanced up to meet the piercing eyes of Skbltz, the tanned and healthy young goat drover (pick a gender). Naturally, the wine was nectar from the gods. But then you shipped home a case and in the cruel light of American day it tasted like pork snot, which, incidentally, is also a delicacy in Phraxistan.

The winery itself is great for learning, but horrendous for objectivity. When you visit wine in its nursery cradle you start to feel protective. Your high standards suddenly feel cruel, as if you were judging your five-year-old's *Orange Juice Can with Macaroni Pavé* through the eyes of *Art in America*. Who, come to think of it, would probably give it a three-page spread.

Producers can be disarming as well. I interviewed one with mesmerizing green eyes on the slopes of Copper Mountain. All day. In the bumps. Late in the afternoon, atop a mountain blanketed in gleaming white fluff against a cobalt sky, he pulled a bottle from his pocket and offered me my first taste of his wares. Ladies and gentlemen of the jury, was that fair?

Restaurants are also tricky. I discover lots of wine there, since my rule is never order something I know. But my tasting notes are peppered with warnings to self: "Objectivity Alert! Swallowing. Lights low. Gorgeous French winemaker!" That sort of thing.

So mostly I taste blind, with all bottles concealed in paper bags. I take very detailed, technical notes on color, smell, mouth-feel, finish and so on, in the constant search to pin down something very slippery. Mostly I work alone, although the company of both geeks and beginners is helpful, because they can always detect things I can't, even if they have no word for it. No, I'm not accepting applications. You freeloader.

I don't usually include descriptions of the wines I recommend. Aside from going stark, raving loony trying to come up with poetic synonyms for acidity each week, the problem is I get only 700 words in the paper. Descriptions would squander them.

Perhaps I'd have the room if, like writer Lane Steinberg, I couched my reviews in Haiku. Here are a few of his examples:

1707 Almansa (Syrah-Cab-Merlot blend) 2002 (Spain)
Here a lousy wine
Passes itself off as good
Oak barrels—big deal

Ironstone Cabernet Franc 2000 (California)
Amazing bouquet!
Beautiful girl, whiny voice
Better as perfume

Panarroz Jumilla 2003 (Spain)
Fat luscious droplets
Another Spanish hat trick
Three grapes & five stars

Gordon Brothers Syrah 2000 (Washington)
A very strange one
Couldn't stand up to dinner
But worked as dessert

Don Aldo Merlot 2000 (Chile)
Funky & skanky
An overripe plum pudding
Left out in the rain

Bodegas Luan Castilla VT "Equis" 2003 (Spain)
A thin, angry wine
A small dog chained to a wall
Good length, but what for?

One.9 (carbs per glass) Merlot 2002 (California)
Like wine that's been raped
A hole cut from its center
For diet Nazis

But I can't help it—I'm wordy. And sometimes my tasting notes need airing, too. Here, then, are some rare notes on a few wines that get me so excited I can't shut up:

Pierre Charlot Château des Chapelains (France)
White Bordeaux is too often stuffy, stuck-up, and boring with a capital B that rhymes with Z that stands for zilch. This one, though, comes on lively and crisp, and has a thing or two to say. Mostly about peaches, pears, and buttery fullness, plus exotic floral and spice tones from a touch of the Muscadelle grape. Then it stops talking. It's wine, after all.

Famiglia Zuccardi Santa Julia Torrontés (Argentina)

I currently have a huge crush on this grape. My heart flutters when I run into it. It's got the heft of Chardonnay, the zing of Sauvignon Blanc and the rosy, orange perfume of Muscat and Riesling. This version from Argentina is sexy, intriguing, and a bargain. Unfortunately, it doesn't know I'm alive.

Schloss Castell Silvaner Trocken (Germany)

Don't let the slab-sided Franken-flask scare you away; I promise there's good wine inside. Dry and slighty spritzy, light on the fruit and flowers, this Silvaner has only 11 percent alcohol, making it the most thirst-quenching drink this side of water.

Viña Peñalolén Sauvignon Blanc (Chile)

Something happens to this normally well-behaved grape when it gets to Chile. It puts down the lap top, strips off the panty hose and morphs into something tropical with shimmying hips and fruit on its head. Without losing its signature muskiness—a scent often elegantly referred to as "cat pee"—this wine explodes in orange, lemon, tangerine and ginger. Until its cell phone rings and breaks the native spell.

Nigl Grüner Veltliner Kremser Freiheit (Austria)

You're knee-deep in a rocky river, fly-fishing in the rain. You're in an ice-cave, shimmering with stalactites. Come back here! You must have been drinking Grüner Veltliner from Nigl. All their wines are winners, but especially the Grüner, which will transport you all the way to Austria for a handful of change.

Castello Montauto Vernaccia di San Gimignano (Italy)

Vernaccia, Verdicchio, Vermentino—who can keep these Italian grapes straight? My wall chart says this should be a light-bodied, delicate wine. But it's lying. Partially barrel-aged, hand-harvested for ripeness, Montauto's version marries perfumes of almond, citrus and lily of the valley with a strikingly rich, dried-fruit maturity in the mouth. Silly chart. You just can't trust inanimate objects these days.

Serra da Estrella Albariño (Spain)

Suddenly über-hip, the Albariño grape from Spain's Rias Baixas region insists on hovering at this higher price-point. Oh, well. Imagine the body and elegance of a greyhound—without the smell. Add lemon-lime, apricot and flowers. Finish with a hint of quinine. Too bad it's all in your imagination. Time to get out of your fantasy world and buy some.

Duval-Leroy Rosé de Saignée NV (France)

For celebrations and seductions, don't waste your money on wines named after a monk. Go for this gorgeous, bone-dry, salmon-colored Champagne. It's packed with strawberry and raspberry aromas, a yeasty complexity that screams France, and bubbles that clock-in about halfway between mousse and gunshot. Instant romance. And more money in your pocket.

Segura Viudas Brut Reserva NV (Spain)

You're a cheapskate. OK, maybe you're just young and poor. Either way, you, too, deserve Champagne. Or the next best thing, Cava. This one has far more flavor and complexity than should be legal at this price. Hide the tag when you pour, and everyone will be convinced you're a high roller. If you quit wearing those Value Village shoes.

Niebaum-Coppola "Sofia" Blanc de Blancs (USA)

Pinot Blanc, Sauvignon Blanc, and Muscat lend muscle, zing and lovely floral notes to this elegant, dry sparkler. Oh, did I mention it comes in a can? A box of four 8-ounce cans, to be precise, each with telescoping bendy straws taped to the side. You might find this embarrassing. All I can say is I've been drinking the stuff all summer.

Reserve St. Martin Merlot (France)

A while back everyone said Languedoc-Roussillon was the region to watch for great wine values. Everyone meaning me, but I didn't have a job with a paper yet, so no one listened, which is good, because few values ever materialized. Here's an exception, a delicious, classic Merlot at an incredible price, with soft cherry and black-berry flavors, and a lush mouth-feel. Now the paper can feel better about hiring me. Maybe they'll even start pay-ing me in cash, instead of bananas.

Castello di Monseran Garnacha (Spain)

Unlike what the giant Australian and American factories pump out for this price, Monseran has personality. It might even have pulchritude, if I knew what it was. Expect a scrumptious mouthful of fruit, plus equal amounts of dusty, earthy, Old World exotica. You'd have to go to Spain for more authenticity at this price. But with airfare and hotel that would come to $1,555.99 a bottle.

Valentin Bianchi Elsa Syrah (Argentina)

The race was tight, with Bianchi's Barbera and Malbec nipping at her heels but Syrah won my heart in the end. Was it the cyclone of red and black berries, the whisper of oak and tannin, or the long, complex finish? Oh, wait; it was a scoring mistake by the South Korean judge. Give 'em all a gold medal.

Banfi Centine (Italy)

I'd make this my house red, if I had a house, but there's no wine rack under this bridge. Lovely blueberry and cherry flavors and a cinnamon-violet nose, plus the tannic umph to keep it serious. The accent's Italian, but show it a steak and it speaks fluent American.

Ricardo Santos Malbec (Argentina)

My Argentinean friend claims Malbec is the sexiest wine of all. This one certainly heats me up. It caresses with silken gloves, feeding you cherries, plums and chocolate. Then you notice darker, savory notes of tar and musk as it attaches the handcuffs. Or it'll switch and let you try. That's what makes it sexy.

Bodegas Muga Rioja Reserva (Spain)

Caution: no-gulping zone. Better send your nose in first to secure the layers of coffee, cedar and ripe cherries. When the coast is clear, let your mouth in for a turn at the summer berries, tobacco and anise. Careful: Despite its medium body, this wine unleashes an unexpected volley of fruit whose impact lasts long after the initial assault is over.

Guelbenzu EVO (Spain)

Guelbenzu is known as a "cult" brand, but that doesn't mean you have to shave your head and accost people in airports to drink it. You just have to look into my eyes and write all your assets over to me. Fine, be that way. While you're at it, check out the ruby red color, raspberry-jam-and-cassis and toasty French oak in this wine. I also found mint, truffles and mocha in there. Now if only I could find my copy of *Extortion for Dummies...*

Terlano "Porphyr" Lagrein (Italy)

Alto Adige, up in the frilly garter atop Italy's boot, has the schizoid character of a border region whose boundaries keep changing. Folk dancers in lederhosen eat caldarroste, as well as "deliziosi krapfen," according to the Town of Terlano website. The Lagrein grape is equally bicultural, combining plummy, spicy, dolce vita sensuality with Teutonic complexity and acid. Boots don't have garters? Shut up and eat your krapfen.

Gaja Ca'Marcanda Magari (Italy)

At this price, a wine better be worth it and this one blew my pants off. I was cold, but happy. You usually find this blend of Merlot, Cab and Cab Franc in a mild-mannered Bordeaux. But, look: boots, tights, a cape, no glasses...it's a Super Tuscan! More powerful than a locomotive, the physique of a body builder, the concentration of an air-traffic controller and the balance of an elephant in high heels crossing Niagara Falls on a tightrope. Guaranteed to save the day.

Recommendations, in the end, are just my opinion. I'm not a machine, but I do weed out the bummers for you. Clearly I'm steadfast in my commitment to objectivity and iron-clad against the lure of sparkling eyes. Well, mostly.

POINTS UNKNOWN
Rating and ranting

WHEN I'M INTERVIEWING WINEMAKERS IN FRANCE, if I wait long enough, they all bring up the same two subjects: the war—still a vivid presence in their lives sixty years after the fact; and über-critic Robert Parker, Jr. Often called the most influential person in wine today, Parker is largely responsible for a world wide upheaval in winemaking. How did he do this? With numbers.

Every day he stands over a sink, tasting, spitting and rating wine from around the globe. He tastes blind, and accepts no gifts. Even his detractors admit he's objective; incorruptible. Possessed of a prodigious palate, he claims to remember every wine he's ever tasted. His feedback reaches far wider than the 40,000 circulation of his newsletter, the *The Wine Advocate*. Yet, he's still one man, with preferences, and that's what gets the wine guys grousing.

On one level, their reaction is simple: If he gives you a low rating, his American, homogenized taste embodies the evils of globalization. But should he grace your wine with the magic numbers—90 to 100—then… Here! Here! It's about time someone shook up those stodgy old châteaux and held them to a standard!

But there's another aspect that miffs these guys. Before Parker, they claim, wine had variety. There were as many different styles as there were fermentation vats. Different countries produced wine with clear differences. Your plonk was someone else's grand cru, and why not? Let a thousand flowers bloom! But the rooty-tooty-fresh-'n-fruity Parker style, they lament, is so fashionable that it's gotten so you can't tell your Jadot from your Jekel. Perhaps coincidentally, the guys I interview, artisans all, invariably say that while *some* winemakers change their style to get Parker ratings, *they* follow their own vision and let the customer decide.

But therein lies the problem. How on earth is the customer supposed to decide? Example: Argonaut Wine and Liquors of Denver stocks 344 different Chardonnays from California alone! Suppose you'd also like to decide about Washington and Oregon, not to mention, oh, Italy, Australia and Spain, for starters? Imagine it was Saturday night and you were going to the movies, only there were 50,000 different films playing at the multiplex. And you're not allowed to read the reviews.

Let the customer decide, indeed! They can say that in France because to the average Frenchman "wine" means "French wine." This is a country where truckers buy splits of Bordeaux at highway rest-stops, golfers chug Burgundy, not Bud, and a glass of red costs less than a medium Coke. Face it, they drink a lot more and know what they like.

But Americans, the kind who don't study vintage-chart flash cards, are faced with a paralyzing array of choices. They can resolve never to venture beyond the few, usually well-advertised, brands they know. Or they can check the ratings. Not just Parker's. Numbers from *Wine Spectator*, *Wine Enthusiast* and *Wine & Spirits* all appear on the shelf-talkers. And what's wrong with that? Doesn't knowing that someone considered it a Best Buy make you feel a little less in-the-dark when coughing up $15-$80 for an unfamiliar bottle?

Perhaps your local movie critic weeps over female bonding, while your tastes run more to female bondage. At least you can read his opinion, even as you take it through a filter. You won't agree with all wine critics, either, but that's no reason to knock the whole concept.

In the best of worlds, you would always have a trusted eno-professional or wine-geek friend help you. Otherwise, letting someone else plough through the business of comparing hundreds of wines for you makes sense, even if the result is rating an artistic creation with a number. Not perfect, but certainly helpful.

OH, ON YOUR WAY, WOULD YOU PICK UP A BOTTLE?
What to bring to dinner

WHEN PEOPLE ASK what sort of wine to bring to someone's house, I always ask, "Is it a doctor?" Doctors—lawyers too, come to think of it—don't so much drink wine as measure with it. A medico I'll call Hans actually prepared me a display of his illustrious empties, presumably so I'd know just how hallowed an esophagus I had the privilege of dining with. I had brought him three fabulous Austrian dessert wines, outrageous bargains all, but as far as he was concerned they might as well have been Yoo-Hoo: He'd never heard of them. Besides, the game was to impress me; he wasn't about to concede a point by being grateful.

For the most part, though, Port, Canadian ice wine and other stickies make great presents—the sort of luxury people deny craving, even as they suck down yours like a truck-mounted Monster Vac.

If the bottle is meant to accompany dinner, however, your best bet is to call and find out what's being served. Then go to a reliable wine shop and ask what pairs well with panko-crusted baby field mice cheeks. They'll be delighted to finally sell that bottle of Hungarian Hárslevelü that most people are too scared to pronounce, much less buy.

But let's say your host's BlackBerry has eloped with his iPod, your carrier pigeon experiences a fatal error and you find yourself winging it. In that case, I recommend Champagne or other sparklers. Their effervescence rubs off on even the dullest crowd and they're versatile enough to surf a four-course meal to shore. The only red that can hope to pull that off is Pinot Noir. It's gone all Hollywood thanks to the fame of *Sideways*, so ought to be not only easily found but much appreciated.

Souvenir wine is appropriate if you're just back from

Tuscany, say, or Minnesota. If the latter sounds doubtful, it's still a good icebreaker—who wouldn't want to hear about the four-day family reunion that drove you out into a blizzard in search of liquor? Lively conversation, after all, is the key to a good evening.

By the same token, when you travel, you can bring wine from home, wherever that home might be. Wine is supposed to speak of place (albeit not with a Brooklyn accent). I still recall a dinner with Russian friends fueled by the sweet, thin, purple goo of their homeland. Yes, grammarians, both friends *and* dinner were operating on a full tank. The result was great hilarity and memories which lasted almost as long as the hangover.

Not everyone is so accommodating. Once I brought a bottle of Zinfandel to a dinner in Normandy. My hostess, Sandra, was a big-shot TV actress with the vermillion mouth and boyish hips and haircut and that make you wonder what queer eye dictates French style. Every morsel of conversation I offered that evening went down in a volley of sophisticated put-downs. As for the wine, Sandra figured if it wasn't made in France, it might as well have come from Russia. She refused to serve it.

So at least it was spared her barbed wit. Most people, though, will praise the wine you bring, out of either insecurity or politeness. I like to thaw things out by inviting criticism: "So, what do you think? Decanter, or smiley-face pitcher?" If your wine turns out to be corked, oxidized or otherwise flawed, try to point this out before someone starts gushing over it, or you'll make them look like an idiot. Unless it's Hans—then be my guest. Or Sandra.

Who was, by the way, within her rights. Hosts are not obliged to serve your swill. The bottle you spent hours choosing could be whisked away to the cellar, as they hand you a glass of white Zinfandel. Be ready to parry this move by holding a second bottle in reserve. Bring your own corkscrew. Fetch an ice bucket or insist on decanting. The idea is an attempted take over of the wine service. This strategy is especially important in a household unaccustomed to wine, where your glass might lie fallow for what feels like a whole growing season.

Control is also key should you discover your pearls are about to be poured to a roomful of swine. You might get away with substituting another bottle for the riff raff. If that's too blatantly selfish, go ahead, be underhanded: Decant your stuff in the kitchen and refill the bottle with plonk to pour at table.

If that's not your style—relax. At least your wine's being tasted. Who knows, you might bring a latent enophile out of the closet. It's not like you're the Chinese importer who was promoting Lafite-Rothschild to restaurant and hotel owners. At a grand reception in Beijing, he had to clam up and watch his clients mix Sprite with the premier cru.

Even that's no tragedy from a Sprite-slugger's point of view. The only true tragedy is wine so expensive—and some cult Cabernets come to mind here—that no one, not even doctors or TV divas dare drink it at all.

CHÂTEAU L'CHAIM
Not your zeyde's kosher wine

MY NEIGHBORS started bringing over meals when I confessed to being so un-domestic as to do my grocery shopping at Office Depot. Since I write with the spontaneity and delight of someone passing a kidney stone, I have to budget my time. Besides, recent experiments (mine) indicate you can meet your short-term nutritional goals adequately with Golden Kernel Deluxe Mixed Nuts and Wint-O-Green LifeSavers. Who needs food groups? They're so collective.

However, when even the tiny bottle of Tabasco that had been with me through marriages, moves and divorces, was empty, I broke down and hit the supermarket. This is a good way to discover what holiday season you're in. Passover's up, with Easter on deck and Mother's Day in the hole. The kosher food display caught my attention. From matzo to borsht it's all made by Manischewitz. Yes, the wine company. Is there a synergy I'm not aware of between vinification and fish-gefiltration? You tell me. Whether you're Jewish, Christian or Wiccan you've tasted their purple treacle. And that's probably your notion of kosher wine.

Surprise, surprise. It's safe to go back to the Seder. Kosher wine has improved enormously. Now, instead of Malaga or elderberry, you can celebrate with well-made Chardonnay, Cabernet and Merlot. What took so long?

From Bacchic gang-bangs to first communion, wine has been lubricating religious rites for eons. It's a stand-in for blood, and even life itself, and opens doorways to that altered mind-state where you converse with God or think you can sing karaoke.

But none of that requires it tastes good. During a Seder, they pour four glasses of wine, to represent four stages of Exodus. But they're generally sipped, not savored. A fifth glass is poured for the Prophet Elijah who typically uses his ghost status as an excuse to avoid drinking it. ("Hey, thanks, I'd love to, but I'm plasma.")

The Concord grape, chosen because of its ubiquity in America, was responsible for the cloying sweetness of past wines. By itself, the grape is acidic enough to pucker your whole face. Only a cru full of sugar makes the medicine go down.

But with better grapes, there's nothing in the process that precludes making good wine. What makes it kosher is that every step, from grape-picking to winemaking to bottling, is supervised by a rabbi and performed only by Sabbath-keeping Jews. No viniculture is allowed from sundown Friday to sundown Saturday, or on religious holidays. Yeast, fining agents and any chemicals that touch the wine must be kosher, and all equipment—barrels, tanks, filters, bottling lines—must be reserved exclusively for kosher use.

Some wines go a step further to become *mevushal*, or immune to contamination by goyishe handlers like waiters and store clerks. This used to be achieved by boiling, which, granted, was a little destructive. Now they use flash pasteurization, which some experts claim actually enhances colors and aromas. True, it can destroy bacteria that help wine age gracefully, but since when is "cellar-worthy" a requirement of Passover wine?

Inconvenient as all that is, wineries have accepted the challenge. Vineyards from Australia to France to Napa are growing noble grapes, under kosher laws, and making sophisticated wine.

As for quality, it depends on the producer. Like all other wines, there's lousy and there's very good indeed. Some kosher Champagne is excellent. Israeli wines take a little getting used to, but it's worth doing. They smell as clearly of the desert as Burgundies do of mulch, and the fruit has a subtle, Old World elegance.

If you're invited to a Seder, do everyone a favor and come bearing decent wine. If you're hosting one, for God's sake don't make your guests suffer. Good kosher wine will kick the joy factor up a few notches. I'm told joy is a requirement of the practicing Jew. And for dessert, I'd recommend a tin of Danish Butter Cookies. You'll find it right between toner cartridges and paperclips.

CHASING COOL
Hippest of the hip

MY EX-HUSBAND, MIKE, has the same five CDs in his car he had when we met twelve years ago. I can recite his grocery list like the pledge of allegiance. When Mike establishes a habit, hurricane force cannot breach his levies. The other night, we're having dinner at his favorite Chinese restaurant, an upscale place, with no splinters in the chopsticks, when Mike starts to order his usual wine, an oak-beglobbed red, once the epitome of high-status, now a sad cliché. Ovaltine would have done a better job of washing down the sweet-sour, firecracker-hot food in front of us. But Mike always orders it because it's the most expensive wine on the list and therefore the best, right?

It's a logical strategy. He's a suave guy. His shirt cuffs are monogrammed. He stands up when you come back to the table from the bathroom. But he's got a lot on his mind, what with making the world safe for country clubs and capitalism. He's too busy analyzing the federal budget to wade through piles of wine literature. How's a guy to keep up?

"Drink what you like!" goes the rallying cry of the anti-snob movement. Sure. Look like an idiot. Humiliate yourself on a date. Take the boss to dinner and order white Zin. Listen, your tastes are your business, but there are times when it's useful to know what the cool crowd is drinking. Consider it a life skill, like tipping, carving a turkey, or fending off stampeding elephants with your umbrella.

Though it's fashionable to pretend otherwise, there are indeed such things as cool and dorky wines. I took the question to an assorted in-crowd of master sommeliers, opinion-making wine press and early adaptors. What wines, I asked, are hotter than hot? What do sommeliers drink and discuss in breathless whispers when they're alone with their own kind?

Here's what I learned. What's *not* cool is money. Forking over wads of cash to have giant, manly, trophy wines decanted is *so* over.

The concept of the moment is *terroir*-wine. Wine from, say, a single, half-acre vineyard on a precipitous mountainside in East Phraxistan. Weeded, harvested, stomped and vinted by one old guy with callused hands and the artistic sensibilities of a concert violinist, and so in tune with life's cycles that the grapes talk to *him*. He has to be into some sustainable-Earth cult involving ancient amphorae, lunar cycles and rune casting. The wine should be quirky, perhaps with a putrid smell you have to get past before you suck it in, gurgle loudly, and proclaim it: "Pretty funky stuff." Funky is good. It speaks of earth and of the fine line between disgusting and delicious. A line the general public, with its bland, corporate taste, is too cowardly to approach.

Cutting-edge regions:

Spain. Hottest of all, and busting out all over with terrific wine. Whites include Albariño from the Rias Baixas (say Bayshez) region and Verdejo and Viura from Rueda. Reds include Tempranillo (in Spain they say "ill-yo," not "eeyo" like you'd expect), Monastrell and Garnacha from Montsant, Priorat, Bierzo, Yecla, Alicante and, well, that's probably enough to write on your cuff for now.

Portugal. Vinho Verde, once just a chugging wine, has gone hip. But the key thing is dry table reds from Douro.

Italy. Like a Fed-Ex guy on meth, Italy just keeps delivering. The hottest regions right now are Friuli and Veneto at the top of the boot, Marches at the calf, Apuglia in the heel, and kicked out in front of the toe, all of Sicily. The hippest grapes are native ones you've never heard of, and Italy's got them up the ying-yang. Start with Lagrein, Fiano, Nero d'Avola, Aglianico and anything beginning with the letter "V."

Germany & Austria. Minerality is a good buzz word to toss around, and you won't go wrong using it on the dry, aromatic whites from these countries. Riesling, Silvaner and Grüner Veltliner are the main players, here.

Hungary. Tokaj is hot as a pistol, both dry wine made from Furmint—a sort of Riesling impersonator—and the legendary dessert wine they've been making since long before it occurred to anyone in Sauternes, whose quality is measured in buckets of sugar, or *puttonyos*. If you happen to live west of New York and east of California you're not going to trip over a lot of this, but it's still good to know.

France. Would you believe...Chablis? This is the in-crowd's version of Chardonnay: steely, minerally, non-oaky and affordable.

Also on the Bus. Sauvignon Blanc from South Africa, Malbec and Torrontés from Argentina, and no doubt a few other wines whose champions will have fired off volleys of outraged emails to me before you even finish this sentence.

Finally, my team of advisors all agree, the hippest wine thing you can do right now is choose screwcaps over corks. A few years back, who woulda thunk it? Cool. It's the new hot. And vice-versa.

PURPLE PASSION
Navigate family gatherings with a bottle and aplomb

LATELY, YOU'VE BECOME VAGUELY AWARE of a pulse deep in your midbrain—a periodic pinch of dread that can mean only one thing: The holidays are upon us! Your subconscious is bracing for the moment when you cross your parents' threshold and feel a great sucking sensation, as years of accomplishment, degrees, promotions and gravitas whoosh out of you, leaving behind a touchy, raw-nerved adolescent, writhing in a state of perpetual discomfort. Ain't family fun?

Winter holidays have long since lost their original purpose, i.e., injecting cheer into a long, dark isolated winter, when crops are in, and there's not much to do except peel hickory nuts and check the woodpile. These days, electricity conquers the dark, cars, planes and email counter the isolation and the concept of nothing to do is so quaint as to be incomprehensible. Yet we're meant to gather together with people we don't really miss and give them more stuff when they've got stuff up the wazoo. Plus, we're supposed to be happy about this, and if we're not, there's something wrong with us. Why don't I care about spraying fake pears with gold paint? Why would I rather find myself in a Soviet gulag than a packed mall, listening to "We Need a Little Christmas" for the 379th time?

Come the revolution, there will be no celebrating except when people break into it spontaneously. Meanwhile, you've got a month of glee ahead. You might as well make the best of it.

This year, though, things will be different. You're bringing the wine. This will brand you a certified adult, which should ease some of your tension. If it doesn't, at least you've got good wine to drown your sorrows in, or perhaps your mom in, if she gets too annoying.

But which wine? There are as many answers to that question as there are albums of family pictures Aunt Bertha's been nagging you to sort through with her.

Unless yours is one of the four gatherings on this planet that actually plans to follow the menu in a foodie magazine (first course: macadamia-yam croutons in a flash-roasted baby haricot-vert purée, paired with a '92 Savigny-les-Beaune), then you've got quite the wine-pairing dilemma.

There are no classic accompaniments. Pizza and Chianti? Inseparable. Oysters and Chablis? A marriage made in...well, not in your family. American holidays are a melting pot of food and cultures, except you don't put everything in a pot and melt it. You put marshmallows on top and melt them.

Consider: dry, salty turkey; sweet, gooey tubers; a cylinder of metallic, red paste that calls itself cranberries. Not to mention the potluck angle. Anyone for sassy pumpkin Jell-O treats? Food to send the bravest wine running home to mama.

And let's not forget the company. I imagine the wine connoisseurship at your celebration ranges from "avoid it" to "swill it." Aunt Kitty sips a little Chardonnay (which is what she calls all white wine now that, for some reason, she's not supposed to call it chablis anymore), Bob, your brother-in-law, drinks manly things like Beer and Red, and Uncle George guzzles vanilla extract in the pantry.

Relax. If you blow it in America, all you have to do is announce that you "take full responsibility." Tap into the pioneer spirit of fearless experimentation and try some of these wine strategies for holiday survival:

Do your relatives absorb wine as fast as your khaki pants absorbed the cranberry sauce your nephew dumped in your lap last year? You'll need to think in terms of value and economy. These days good wine comes in boxes, tetra packs and jugs. One school of thought goes that too much booze turns a grudge-fest into a slug-fest. I'm of the school that if you can't enjoy family adversity, you should have the option of blotting it out. Don't be stingy.

Celebrate diversity. Open bottles of red and white, set them out and let people choose for themselves.

If you're the family peacemaker, you're tempted to negotiate détente between white and red drinkers. Instead, why not split the difference with lighter, elegant reds like Pinot Noir and Beaujolais. Refreshing enough to wash down great lumps of creamed onions and mashed potatoes, they can also hold their own against the most muscular gravy. There was a time when Pinot Noir was too expensive to waste on a crowd. Besides, it's subtle, something that could hardly be said of your family. But since it seems to be turning into the new red generic, it's a good bet.

You're a card-carrying, Bordeaux-hoarding wine snob. So what. Some of your relatives won't even mess with wine unless it's sweet. Put them over the moon with something sweet and fizzy, like Moscato or Prosecco. Both Riesling and Gewürztraminer come dry and semi-sweet. They're great foils for bizarre food and excellent for placating the Cabal of White

Zindaliers that lurks in even the finest families. They also have the advantage of being relatively low in alcohol, which could avert some nasty family scenes.

But sometimes higher alcohol is just what the doctor ordered. If that's your family, think Zinfandel: whoppingly alcoholic with loads of luscious fruit to cosy up to and none of those nasty tannins. It's also the patriotic thing to do; the only serious wine grape that's American. Never mind that forensic viticulturists are forever trying to prove that it's second-clone-once-removed from the national grape of Blatybutskaya. What's important is that no other country grows Zinfandel, so for all intents and purposes it's ours.

Do your family gatherings ring with the joie-de-vivre of a tax audit? You need bubbles. They'll make you feel more buoyant and your relatives seem more interesting. Plus, food wise, there's hardly a meal you couldn't happily tackle with only sparkling wine.

But rather than limit yourself to the usual Champagne or Cava, check out sparkling Shiraz. If you're never heard of it, join the club. Long a favorite in Australia, it's almost unknown here. Imagine marrying the plummy, dry masculinity of Shiraz (Syrah) with the effervescence of Champagne. Neither could I until I tried it. Wow! The first sip is startling, like Julie Andrews segueing into "Louie Louie." But you get used to it quickly. Served chilled, it's deliciously refreshing with food, while delivering the structure and substance that real men crave. Versatile, shockingly different, a wine everyone seems to love.

When you're armed with good wine, neither family feud nor psychological regression can touch you. You might even find yourself downright cheery. But when you start gilding pinecones it's time to lay off the stuff.

Part 9
The Restaurant Experience

AS IF HASHING IT OUT in relative anonymity at the store weren't hard enough, now you have to perform this wine-choosing stunt in front of a roomful of people! Fear no more. Armed with this book, next time you're in a restaurant and the supercilious wine waiter starts sneering, just whip it out and clonk him over the head!

THE SOM-WHISPERER
Get him eating out of your hand while you drink out of his

AS A BABE OF THREE, I liked sitting on my mother's naked stomach and playing a game I called "Does This Hurt?" She didn't much care for it, but I had burning questions to answer, like, "What happens if you twist these?"

Curiosity is still my master. I'm a founding member of Googlers Anonymous. My interviews are compared unfavorably with the Spanish Inquisition. But it serves me well in restaurants. Ask the right questions, I've learned, and you need never settle for wine you don't love. My table ends up a forest of glasses; I taste dozens of wines that never appear on the check.

"Sure," you say, "but you're a wine critic. What about the rest of us?" Actually, most of the world, including, I suspect, the newspaper I write for, has no clue who I am. The routine I'm

147

about to share with you works whether I reveal my identity or not.

For purposes of assisted social suicide, there's nothing quite like the sommelier appearing out of the gloom with his trademark wine list and sickle. But you can harness his powers for the good. Don't worry about sounding like a newbie. The tip-top echelons of winedom—marcheses, masters of glass, heads of wine industry—*all* ask questions of the sommelier. Because no matter who the grand funkety-funk you are, the som has tasted wines you haven't. Why not benefit?

Skip the nervous laugh and declaration of ignorance. Do you act this way with the telephone tech support guy in Afghanistan who's trying to determine why your computer keeps spewing hot chicken soup out of its serial port? Certainly not. You go along with the program: "You see the little button at the top of your screen that says XMpptss&^%$? No? OK, let's start again. You sure it is a computer and not a toaster?"

Good sommeliers are a font of information. At the highest levels, the Master Som spends years cramming for the vinous equivalent of law boards. All that knowledge, building up pressure in his brain! You will act as a release valve, transitioning him to a calm, pleasurable brain state. He will want to keep returning to your table to get more of this drug that is you. Here's what to say:

"Who writes the wine list?" This person can reveal to you hidden gems. But first, whether tiny table tent or a ten-ton tome, you must compliment it. "How refreshing! An all-Retsina theme!" you might exclaim.

"Do you get to taste a lot of these wines?" Positive spin. "How cool!" the question says, "How unlike those stupid restaurants that don't care a fig for empowering their staff. You, in contrast, are Super Som!"

Alternative phrasing:

"Do they taste you through a lot of these wines?" You speak the lingo; you might be in the business.

Discuss the dishes you've chosen and anything else relevant such as you're into Spain or you prefer big and fruit-juicy to austere and intellectual. Find a region, grape or term you don't know much about and ask some version of:

"What's up with that?" You may learn why Sauvignon Blanc tastes like cat pee in New Zealand, if there's really any good Merlot, or whether Chianti Classico is a *region* or *type* of Chianti. Pretty soon it's time for:

"What do you recommend?" He needs a price range, so point to a number on the list and say, "Something like that." Don't worry if it's low. What do you suppose *they* drink at home? Besides, at that price, you might order more bottles. Now it's time to deploy the Magic Question:

"What about you? What are you passionate about?" And just like that, you are no longer a bland, faceless customer. You have become an adventurous spirit, one of his tribe. What's more, you *care* about *his* tastes. The rewards are twofold. You will encounter the hippest, cutting-edgest of wines—something wonderful and wild that could never come from a factory. Plus, get a som cranked up enough about his baby and sooner or later he will be compelled to utter the phrase you've been waiting for:

"No, really! I'm so sure you're going to love it that if you don't, I'll take it back!"

Which he will, and drink with pleasure in the kitchen. This phrase disarms the whole rejection issue. Wine should be sent back only if flawed. Never, a) to show what a big shot you are or b) because you just don't like it. Now that you've engaged the som, however, you're free to say, "Hey, thanks for trying, but I really can't get into this."

Assuming you do like it, though, always offer both som and waiters a taste. This is courteous and useful for them. Plus it injects some fun into their long, exhausting night of work. Don't worry about "giving away" your wine. This move will repay itself many times over. Especially if you launch the bonus question:

"**If you happen to open something that would help me learn more, and I could get just a tiny taste of it, I'd really appreciate the opportunity.**" Offer to pay, of course, but you seldom will. If they go for it, a funny thing happens. Once they start, they can't stop. You'll be offered tastes of everything from Pinot to Perrier. You must be extremely gracious, polite and thankful. And always tip handsomely for this sort of experience.

At a restaurant dinner in New York featuring wine critic Robert Parker Jr., I offered a copy of my book, *Waiter, There's a Horse in My Wine*, to a gentleman at my table. "Learn about wine," I suggested, "while spitting it out your nose laughing." With a patronizing little smile and nod, he answered, "I don't think so, dear. I already *know all* about wine." Which doesn't say much for Mr. Parker, who read his copy cover-to-cover on the plane to France and wrote back nice things about it. But then I'll bet that man's mom never had to play *Come in Tokyo*.

BOUTEILLE CALL
How 'bout a $9 wine on the list?

A COMMON REFRAIN SUNG BY PEOPLE who make or sell wine is that Americans should drink it more like Europeans, namely, at every meal that doesn't involve Cheerios. (Try a Vouvray to balance the oaty richness.)

If we don't lubricate our lunch, perhaps it's because American wines, which can pack up to twice the alcohol of their Euro counterparts, are more likely to lead to afternoons of napping than of working. Another reason is price. Compared to iced tea or bottled water, wine is a luxury here, while a glass of house white in a European café costs no more than a Coke. You won't swirl it or be transfixed by profundity, but it's usually decent. And if not, so what? You're not out the

$6 to $18 that a glass of wine sets you back stateside.

Fred Franzia of the Bronco Wine Company wants to change this. His Charles Shaw label, AKA Two Buck Chuck, set off a stampede when Trader Joe's began selling it for $1.99 a bottle. Taking advantage of the recent grape glut, Franzia bottles pleasant, drinkable wine—Merlot, Chardonnay and the usual suspects—at amazing prices. His other value labels include Crane Lake, Salmon Creek and Dona Sol, but Chuck is clearly the star, selling over ten million cases in two years. Other wineries have leapt into the "ultra-value" category he created, including Palamon, a California Cab sold at Sam's Clubs, and Lost Vineyards, who bottle up surplus from Spain, Portugal and Argentina.

Even connoisseurs like to keep something around for everyday purposes. Europeans sometimes tap a basement keg. These wines offer a respectable alternative to the jug or box.

The rest of the industry is worried: Is this bringing in new drinkers, or just cannibalizing more expensive sales? While they cogitate, Franzia has dropped another bomb, this time a challenge to restaurants: How about a wine on the list for under ten bucks? His Salmon Creek line, for example, which wholesales for $2 to $4 a bottle.

Three times wholesale is standard restaurant mark up, but other voodoo goes into price decisions and restaurants vary considerably. Customers will graciously pay a premium for service, atmosphere and not having to go shopping and do the dishes. Yet wine markups can be hard to swallow. The cost of food, with all its ingredients, labor and transformation, is tricky to compare with what you'd make at home. But $30 for a bottle that costs $10 in the store down the block is easy to spot. It's not much better in states that let you bring your own bottle, when restaurants like Napa's trendy French Laundry see fit to charge $50 for corkage, or in this case, screwage.

Would you order a $9 wine? Restaurants who have taken

the challenge report great sales and happy customers. Yet few will even test drive the concept. Salmon Creek runs $20–$25 on wine lists in Colorado, my home state. The excuse is that no one orders wine under $16, for fear it will be rubbish. Until recently, it probably was.

But restaurants are excellent Sherpas when it comes to new trends. Just as they lure patrons out of their Chardonnay comfort and into the wild, world of New Zealand Sauvignon Blanc, they could explain that this is not your grandpa's nine-buck wine. They could transform the wine-wary, and goose the type that saves wine for special occasions. In short, they could normalize the stuff!

But, back here on earth, restaurants are not exactly stampeding for the privilege. So I'm deputizing you, instead. Armed with Franzia's challenge and privy to the low wholesale price, your mission, if you spot Salmon Creek on a wine list (it's not available in stores) is to demand justice! A sit-in would be nice. If you find a restaurant bold enough for the $9 challenge, let me know.

GET LUCKY
You are what you drink

AH, THE FIRST DATE! Candy wrappers and coffee lids gathered up and banished from your car. You walk the extra yards to open the passenger-side door, your gait stiffened by the chafe of brand new underwear. Not yet synched in the rhythms of a couple, the two of you bump and apologize your way into a restaurant and settle awkwardly into a booth and a self-consciously upbeat conversation, until the waiter comes by, thank God, to take your bar order. What are you drinking?

If you want to get lucky, skip the Ketel One and order Australian wine, says a recent survey. Fifty-three percent of singles favored dates who pick Aussie over orderers of Russian vodka (18 percent), Belgian beer (15 percent) or Port (14 percent). Upside-down margaritas, I presume, were not an option. For optimal results, spend the night before cramming: 72 percent agreed that wine knowledge made a member of the opposite sex more attractive. (That would explain the line of guys outside my door—and all this time I thought they were just intercepting wine samples!) Not surprisingly, men were more likely than women to claim such knowledge. Singles also admitted using wine to buff up their own image, deliberately opting for it over beer, soda or 'tinis on a first date. Eighty-three percent thought it upped the love quotient, coloring a normal evening romantic.

Fine, you'll order wine, but why Australian? Apparently the flag you wave reveals as much about you as your handwriting, ink blots or TiVo schedule. Selecting *en Français* brands you an incorrigible snob, according to 76 percent of respondents. Vino Italiano says sexy (40 percent) and stylish (37 percent), while a visit to Oz deems you adventurous (62 percent) and fun (32 percent).

Whoa, there! What's wrong with sexy and stylish? When an eel bites your knee as you swim in the sea that's a moray, right? Why sweat the REI climbing wall on a first date? Because when participants were asked to rate the most important characteristic in a perspective mate, 63 percent chose fun. Maybe you're not looking to mate for life and produce fertile offspring. Perhaps you're just hoping for an evening of body-and-fender work, as my father used to put it. You might even resonate to the phrase my ex whispers fondly in my ear: "Marriage is temporary, but divorce is forever."

But if you're braced for the long haul, locked and loaded for meeting the parents, go with Australian. And, unless you're a statistical deviant, chances are you already do: the 47 percent of men and 59 percent of women unwilling to spend more than

$25-a-bottle on the first date don't leave themselves much *but* Australia to choose from.

Not that that's a bad thing. Two points the survey didn't mention: first, Australian wines tend to be idiot-proof—full of fruit, smooth and easy drinking. You can even pronounce them! Second, their alcohol content is relatively high, which is relevant if you're softening up your date or agreeing to something that didn't seem like a good idea a few hours ago.

Before you bid farewell to Barolo or Burgundy, however, you might just wonder wonder who wrote this particular book of love. The survey was designed and administered by the Australian Wine Board in concert with Match.com, the "global leader in on-line dating."

This just goes to show that:

a) Anyone can design a poll working backward from desired results.

b) People on first dates are liars. Before you know it they're spilling coffee on the gear shift, letting the car door slam in your face and sporting hole-riddled undies of washer-tinted gray. But who cares? The fun will last forever.

WINGING IT
Wine service in the skies

AS A FREQUENT FLYER ON UNITED, I get a glimpse of the good old days when kings were kings and serfs were scum. Singapore Air, by contrast, takes all the fun out of it by giving slippers and toothbrushes—formerly a First Class perk—to economy fliers. What's the point of earning all those miles if you can't lord it over the masses?

But even Premier Execs get the blues. A last minute booking finds me crammed with the hordes in Economy Minus. At least I have a window. "We're expecting a full flight…" bleats the loudspeaker. And when are they not? Armed with laptop, earplugs and sandwich, what I need now is some wine.

Remember when airplanes were magic portals to exciting new worlds and travelers guzzled full-blooded Mary instead of just the mix? Now that they're just another commute, no one seems to be drinking.

At eight p.m., I'm the only drinker for rows around. Requesting two mini bottles of white makes me feel like a crazed lush. The stigma is palpable, as if the whole cabin's bracing for me to burst into song, dance and loud complaints or drop my pants for the flight attendant's enjoyment.

It's different up front, I think, wistfully. There, wine just keeps getting better. Airlines hire big-name gurus to choose it. Magazines rate it. International flights feature real Champagne, as well as selections from Burgundy, Bordeaux, Provence, the Rhône and the Rhine.

My friend Doug Frost, one of the few people in the world to achieve both Master Sommelier and Master of Wine status, also has the distinction of being crowned United Airlines' Sommelier in the Skies. There, he has a more challenging job than his earth-bound colleagues. Just imagine the logistics of 75 different wines, ranging from ten dollar Aussie Shiraz to grand cru Champagne, in warehouses around the world.

The first duty of a flying wine is to be sturdy and balanced, so it can survive the temperature changes, movement and turbulence of travel. The chemistry of flight presents triple trouble: at 30,000 feet, hypoxic stress and hormonal changes play tricks on the taste buds, making sugar, salt and metallic flavors stand out and acid and tannins seem harsher.

When you de-plane in a damp climate, you smell a rush of trees, earth and people. Humidity carries scent. Cabin air, however, is woefully arid. Aromas that scream at sea level barely whisper in a plane.

Then there's the business of alcohol. A wonderful carrier

of flavor and aroma, alcohol also packs a mean punch at altitude. So it's off-limits for upping the taste ante.

So Doug looks for low-acid, low-tannin, fruit-forward wines, with big, juicy aromas—precisely what Americans like to drink.

Business and First Class mystique demands corks. Back here in domestic steerage, where choice is limited to red or white, you get single serving bottles with screwcaps. That's cool with me—at least I'll get clean wine, free of problems like TCA or oxidation. Or so I think. But bottle #1 pours out with the deep yellow tinge of a urine sample and smells like acrid sherry. Cooked. Probably on some runway in the sun.

So then I start wondering—should I send it back? The beverage cart has moved on down the aisle. I'm fenced in by a guy asleep in the middle seat and a girl on the aisle engrossed in the film. Do I raise my hand and complain? Press the call button?

I imagine the reaction: "What do you know about wine? You're economy!" they'd sneer. But if I whipped out my boarding pass stub… "Oh, goodness, a Premier Executive! So sorry, ma'am! Please wait while we fetch a jeroboam of Dom Perignon!"

Attendants are supposed to accept the wine opinions of flyers, Doug tells me. They don't get a ton of wine training themselves, what with learning the seatbelt buckling pantomime, and how to emphasize the wrong words, as in "we *will* be taxiing to the gate *for* a few more minutes…"

As for alternatives in the cheap seats, the rule, as in so many things, is ask nicely and nice things may happen. Kindly attendants have been known to smuggle you a glass from the snob section if you're desperate.

In the end, all I do is pour the bad stuff back in the bottle to free my plastic cup. Bottle #2 pours out pale straw with faint whiffs of oak, like a well-behaved, generic Chardonnay should. You get what you pay for. If you're flying for the wine, upgrade.

MIDNIGHT AT THE OASIS
The blindest of tastings

"YOUR WINE GLASS IS ON THE RIGHT, your water on the left. Bon appetit." That's all we're told before they leave us in total darkness, or, in this case, *Dans le Noir*, a restaurant in Paris that gives new meaning to the concept of blind tasting.

Enter the brightly-lit bar, crammed with young trendies, and you could be in any urban restaurant. Except there's an alcove for seeing-eye dogs. And they confiscate cell phones, watches and anything else luminous and suggest you visit the john now or forever hold your piss.

We order before entering the dining room. My date opts for the surprise menu. Then our waitress emerges from within. Caroline has beautiful chocolate skin, meticulous cornrows and eyes that roll up in her head. She's blind. "Put your hand on my shoulder and follow me," she says, and leads us through a curtain into pitch darkness. "We're turning right, now left. Feel these two tables? Go between them and sit down." I sink onto a bench and right away realize someone is sitting next to me. The voice reveals a girl. I presume seating is carefully arranged to minimize groping; after all, we're in France. Infrared cameras monitor the room, in case of a complaint.

Total dark makes some people claustrophobic. Waiters spend as much time calming nerves as serving. Diners around us are talking a little too loudly—whistling, as it were, in the dark, and bonding across tables, in their common disorientation, with strangers in the night.

I find the blackout peaceful and oddly familiar. Like dreaming. My mind's eye vividly populates the void with tables, waiters and walls. I ponder how people who are born blind go about mentally organizing the space around them. Conversation is difficult for me; without eye contact my attention keeps drifting off. I catch myself in bizarre listening postures; cranked way

157

over to one side, chin and eyes aimed at the invisible ceiling. Then I remember the infrared camera and snap to attention.

The restaurant grew from a project of the Paul Guinot Society, formed just after World War I to promote culture, sports, policy and jobs for the blind. *Le Goût du Noir* (Taste of the Dark) was a series of blind soirées meant to jolt people out of their normal preconceptions through the shock of role reversal. Most of us, paralyzed by political correctness—do you pity? offer help?—have little contact with the blind. But here, in their kingdom of darkness, they are your Boy Scout leader, Sherpa and life line.

The restaurant employs twelve full-time blind waiters. It also hosts debates, dating nights, business meetings, and inevitably—in a setting that, stifling one sense, puts the others on orange alert—wine tastings. I'd been looking forward to an extra-sensory wine experience. Alas, our wine, once I manage to get as much into the glass as I spill on the table, is breathtakingly awful. Contemplating a new low in the annals of wine-snobbery, I ponder: Do you send a bottle back in a blind restaurant? Yes! For once, I'm glad to know a waiter's name. I call out to the all-powerful Caroline who is instantly by my side. The replacement bottle is scarcely better.

Food is another story. After a tentative stab or two, I dispense with the fork. Like a golf club, it's clearly way too long for meaningful contact with its target. Instead, I plunge right in and violate all the etiquettes of societies that eat with their hands, using left and right indiscriminately and licking my fingers. Flavors burst alive. I'm struck by the startling beauty of juxtaposing sweet and salt, the heartrending poignancy of the savory flavor known as umami, represented here by grilled eggplant whose crunchy crust gives way to a meltingly creamy center.

I have my own little hedonistic orgy, dripping bits of fish and fruit into my mouth like a bit-player from *Caligula*. I became so deeply involved with the chocolate-hazelnut mousse

I'm supposed to be sharing that my date never learns of its existence. Oh, well. Out of sight, out of mind.

DON'T EAT WHILE I'M TALKING TO YOU
Annoying waiters and the customers who stiff them

WE INTERRUPT OUR REGULAR WINE COLUMN to bring you an irritating restaurant trend. Normal, cheerful wine attitude will return next week.

The problem is over-eager servers, constantly interrupting to find out if everything's OK, which it would be except for their interruptions to find out if everything's OK. It's like waking you up to ask how you're sleeping.

When did waiters start barging into conversations? They stride right over your punch line in order to introduce themselves and describe dishes already explained in the menu. They loom at your shoulder with great phallic cylinders, asking if you wouldn't like *freshly ground* pepper or cheese, as if the rest of your dish came out of a can. May they light your candle? Are you enjoying your appetizer? Your entrée? Your wine? Would you like to see the dessert menu? (Might as well yell, "Fat slob alert!" Just bring the damn thing.) And on they fuss, too busy attending to your needs to notice you don't have any. Except, perhaps, the need to resurrect the thread and mood of a besieged conversation.

They fight you for your plate before you're finished. "Are you still working on that?" and then whip it away fast enough to serve the same steak to three different tables a night. Eventually you yield, beaten and too shamed to chew. The spread-knife-and-fork symbol used to keep them at bay, but evidently this new breed of super waiters is immune to its power.

They announce their personal favorite dishes, like you care, and then say "Good choice!" when you make one, leaving other diners to wonder what *they* ordered: the salmonella surprise? I don't want a waiter with tastes. I don't want a waiter with personality and a name and a shoe size. I want a server: efficient, invisible, unobtrusive, who stays mum until I deign to acknowledge him, and then glides occasionally by to make eye contact, just in case.

I pay a masseuse so I don't have to rub back. I don't take my doctor's temperature. At restaurants I don't do the dishes, the cooking, or the clearing up, and I pay for the exquisite illusion that, for this hour, at least, my needs are all that matter. Then I go back to real life where my boss doesn't care if I broke a tooth or got depressed or lost my laptop—only that I deliver by deadline.

As long as I've worked up this head of steam, and considering this is a wine column, I'll take a swipe at some all-too-common problems with wine service. Like bringing a different vintage from the one on the list, a frequent bait-and-switch maneuver. I catch it just enough to know how often I probably miss it.

Lukewarm reds—room temperature if you happen to live in a sweat lodge—are about as refreshing as Kaopectate and make you wonder what changes life above the stove has wrought. Over-chilled whites are rarer and you can always cuddle the glass to warm them, but with your own hands, please; more and more servers pick your glass up when they pour, sometimes by the bowl, leaving smudgy forensics between you and your vino.

Others angle for a re-order by emptying an entire bottle at once into three or four glasses. Rim-high wine gets the pouring business over with quickly, but makes smelling impossible and spilling inevitable.

Hoarding the crystal is false economy and comes off as hostile. I break enough at home to understand saving the Riedels for customers who care. But that doesn't include only buyers of expensive wine. Anyone who asks for a glass upgrade should get it.

If wine is corked, oxidized or otherwise ruined, you shouldn't need a court order to send it back. Servers who haven't learned to recognize these faults should at least be told they exist. I don't *like* sending wine back. But I wouldn't pay for food that was spoiled, either.

My toughest wrangle was in a restaurant in the heart of Beaune, Burgundy. To the horror of my French dining companion, I got in an argument with the native waiter over whether our wine was cooked. Finally, snootily, as only the French can snoot, the waiter brought us a fresh bottle, drawing upon an extraordinarily broad repertoire of smirks as he uncorked it. Later in the meal, though, he came back and if he had had a tail it would have been between his legs as he told us the chef was in agreement with *la folle Américaine*. I've got to give the guy credit, though: after that he made himself scarce. And never, once, did he tell us that his name was Gaston and he would be our waiter this evening.

Part II—Waiter's Revenge

"Drink your precious wine until you puke your guts out and the sweeping staff carry your carcass away."

"Use the buffet line and keep your yap shut."

Just some of the nicer responses to the column I wrote about overeager servers. Frustrated customers outnumbered irate waiters three to one, but sparks flew from both sides. Diners were fed up with over-intimate waiters interrupting, annoying, "Killing us with service," as well as with "Wait staff who want to become the star of your evening."

One diner writes: "I don't really care what your name is—I assume you will be my waiter as you are standing next to my table with a pad and pencil waiting to take my order."

Another concludes, "If a waitperson can't tell when a customer is through, perhaps a career change is in order."

Most had known wonderful service; waiters who "Never

asked 'how are we doing?' or 'do you need anything?' because they observed the table and *knew*. In other words, a pro."

Waiters disagreed. "Your concept of what a server should be is novel at best, as well as arrogant." Furthermore, they scolded, "Servers are *not* mind readers, much as you would like them to be."

Clearly, I was a pompous jerk: "I can only assume by the way that you view servers as being completely beneath you, that you usually leave much less than the standard gratuity."

They're dead wrong. I've done my share of waiting. A quick examination of the "gratuity" line on my enormous pile of Visa receipts will attest to my respect for the profession. Yet many felt the concept of ego-less serving was demeaning: "Please keep in mind that these people are servERS not servANTS. Just because they are waiting on you is no excuse to be outright rude." I'm not quite sure I get the difference, but I can't see a reason to be rude to either. One manager has to constantly remind his staff: "Humility does no damage to my manhood, self-respect, or job satisfaction. I make my living by being a font of knowledge…and giving that knowledge up when appropriate—like when I am asked!"

In Europe, the profession of waiter is a respectable one. Hell, most people are terrified of the haute cuisine staff in Paris. But America's servers want it clear this is only a temporary gig:

"In the future, be nice to us. We're just humans, doing the best we can and many of us might be having lunch with people like you some day!"

They decried being treated "Like they do not exist as human beings and as intelligent people who are not only integral members of our society, but many of us are or will be great contributors to the arts and humanities of the world."

No doubt. But that's a different role. When you star as Hamlet, I hope you're not going to remind us of the ringtones included with your new wireless plan.

I expected gripes, but was surprised at the fury and self-righteousness: "I have been rude to those who I believed deserved it, and I have verbally shot customers down when they tried to look impressive for their companions at my expense. No regrets. Woe to diners who dared touch the wine bottle—Until you've paid the check, it's not yours."

Or mistook cordiality for friendship—"Stop inviting us to your house. It's never going to happen. The last thing we want to do on our day off is anything that reminds us of work."

Whence this bitterness, I wondered, plucking another arrow from of my behind. Then I read: "Your server has no control over temperatures of wine, vintages and glassware—cut them some slack and pass your concerns on to the manager." And: "See how much fun it is to be expected to sell and up-sell at every chance, then be given a two-dollar tip because your customer thought you were 'obtrusive.'"

Suddenly, I got it. The biggest beefs of customers—from hurry-up table turning to fireworks that pass for service—are all management decisions. Waiters, caught in the middle, are feeling the squeeze. Imagine squatting on your haunches, scribbling your name in crayon on the placemat as per National Crab-n-Chick's training manual, and finding yourself eye to eye with a connoisseur of fine dining. Or dutifully cramming the day's specials, only to encounter this fellow:

"He had to recite his litany of menu items and cut me off and gave a seemingly endless list of 'specials,' none of which I wanted. God knows how long it took him to memorize—I was actually impressed—but also annoyed."

The gulf between what diners want and what management delivers is a puzzlement deserving its own column. Waiters, meanwhile, as the last link between kitchen and mouth, will continue to field the complaints. To those who do it with grace and pride: I salute you.

Part 10

Eating & Drinking

OH, YEAH, REMEMBER FOOD? That stuff you chew between gulps of wine? I don't like to tell you what goes with what, because I think that's the business of your own personal mouth. Yet no wine book is complete without a section about food. At least as a supporting player. Its agent kept calling. What could I do?

MATCHMAKING
Pairing wine and food

YOU EAT FOOD. You drink wine. But just try to do it together! Advice on the subject is as reassuring as a picnic on quicksand. There are contradictions: "Balance a heavy cream sauce with a full-bodied wine, or cut through it with a thin, acidic one!" Leaps of extrapolation: "Since Chenin Blanc goes with oysters, and Pinot Noir with roast chicken, then obviously: Grenache and curried lamb!" Improbable pairings: "Serve this wine with wild king salmon ceviche and a white truffle risotto." Right. Every Tuesday.

How important is wine and food pairing? You could devote your life to it, but dinner won't be ruined if you don't. Do you choose Coke over Mountain Dew to complement the organoleptic properties of your Whopper? Then you probably won't be shot for ordering the wine and food you want without considering their cohabiting arrangements.

They rarely rendezvous in your mouth, anyway. You probably eat a bite or two, and then sip some wine for the same reason you drink water—to refresh and lubricate. After the initial tasting is over, most of us segue into eating and drinking and forget all about the match.

Having said all that, it's useful to understand something about what wine and food do to each other. Perhaps you're afraid you'll be brought before the wine-crimes tribunal if you order wrong. Or you don't want to serve that '82 Latour with something that makes it taste as worthless as your spouse thinks this whole linen-closet-to-wine-cellar construction project is. Besides, if you're the least bit scientific, or you just like making odd noises and playing with your food, experiments can be fun.

Acidic wines are refreshing and easy to pair. Alcoholic wines are neither. Harsh tannins, as in a young Cabernet, smooth out dramatically with a little protein or fat. Just about all food tastes better with just about any wine.

We're supposed to scoff at the old "red with meat, white with fish" dictum. But it's really just a way of saying that when food and wine are unequal in power, the weaker loses. If you put Pavarotti in the middle school choir, how do you suppose your 'tween will sound? Actually, oomph counts for more than color. A big, fat, white like Chardonnay can take on a porterhouse without breaking a sweat. Lighter reds with low tannins couldn't hope to smother a swordfish. Sauce often trumps animal. Salmon and chicken, those all-terrain vehicles for sauce, are pretty much AC/DC.

A few foods pose problems only a trained, toque-bearing chef should address. Asparagus and artichokes, for example, have as distinct an effect on wine as they do on your own bodily fluids. Mint makes you odor-blind, which is why coroners rub it under their noses. No wine is welcome when your tongue has been Brazilian bikini waxed by hot peppers. Spicy food—Thai, Indian or Mexican—cries out for sweet, acidic refreshment. This is why God gave us margaritas. No one ever wasted away again in Tempranilloville.

The "When in Tijuana" strategy is, in fact, a good one. Regional wines evolve hand in hand with local food; it's a sound bet they complement one another. You go to Luigi's for *straccoto* not grits, so what's with the Napa Merlot? Order Brunello!

If there is entrée anarchy at your table, go for the diplomats: Pinot Noir and Champagne. Pinot, the red grape of Burgundy, has the good manners to play nicely with everything from flounder to ribs, while Champagne, despite its party-girl reputation, can behave itself all the way from appetizer to dessert.

If you forget all of this, have faith in your own intuition, which isn't too shabby. Somehow you know that pickles, ketchup and cheese go with a hamburger, but Hershey's syrup does not. You'll do just fine.

AMAZING ALCHEMY
Wine in the kitchen

COOKING WITH WINE is not just for Cable-network chefs and metrosexual sushi-folders. Even a serial defroster can parlay a few pours into gourmet wizardry. Guys like cooking with wine and woman know it. Dumping Chianti into spaghetti sauce in college was the seminal moment for many a later chef. Alas, women who encourage this probably never anticipate how many pots and pans the future toque will leave for them to wash.

It's hard to go wrong with wine in the kitchen as long as you obey the cardinal rule: Don't cook with anything you wouldn't drink. Forget supermarket "cooking wine." It's highly salted and an insult to any dish. Nix as well the open bottle languishing in the back of your fridge. Wine concentrates as it cooks, so any hints of oxidation or vinegar will permeate in the end.

Chefs may tout the complexity of European wines versus the fruity obviousness of the New World, but even they don't much enjoy pouring a $50 bottle into the stewpot. So while you can cook with the same wine you're going to drink, if it's old or precious, opt for something decent but cheaper in the same grape family.

Wine's kitchen talents include:

1. Deglazing: After sautéing, say, a breaded veal medallion, remove it to a plate, add wine to the pan while still on the flame and use a spatula to scrape the crunchy bits stuck to the bottom. They'll come up easily and, along with the wine, will form the basis of a sauce.

2. Reducing: For a great accompaniment to steak or fish, sauté shallots or mushrooms in wine over low heat until all liquid is absorbed. Partway through, stir in as many sticks of butter as your Atkins delusions permit.

3. Marinating: The alcohol and acid in wine break down tough fibers in meat, tenderizing and bringing out its flavor. If you want to use the marinade for a sauce as well, boil it for a few minutes to kill any bacteria left from the raw meat.

4. Steaming: Vegetables, fish and potatoes can all be cooked by the vapor of wine rather than water. To rev up a bland preparation, pick aromatic wine or season it with herbs.

5. Poaching: A low-fat option that's microwave friendly. Pour white wine and seasonings over fish or vegetables like asparagus or broccoli in a Pyrex pan or bowl and zap on high for a couple of minutes.

6. Braising: Long, slow cooking to break down the fibers in tough but flavorful cuts of meat. Think coq au vin or bœuf bourguignon—falling off the bone comfort food. The key is hours of simmering—a Crock-Pot is ideal—followed by a day of mellowing in the fridge to focus and concentrate flavors before the final reheating and additions.

7. Infusing: For moistness and flavor, use a syringe with a thick needle to infuse meat before cooking. A wonderful combo is roast chicken or turkey shot through with Riesling. While you're playing doctor, try filling the inside cavities of giant, mutant strawberries with liqueur.

8. Flambéing: After browning anything from boneless chicken breasts to bananas, add wine to the pan, heat a large metal spoon of same over a flame until it catches fire and then toss it in the pan and watch the flames rise. Then put out the curtains. Besides the drama, flambéing adds wine's perfume while quickly burning away its alcohol.

But then pretty much any cooking method does that, since alcohol evaporates at a lower temperature than water, which means you can cook with wine for both dry adults and sophisticated children. Just don't serve uncooked boozy dishes like babas au rhum or fruitcake. Some recipes call for, say, a teaspoon of brandy, but give the option of substituting vanilla extract, presumably to keep the thing alcohol-free. But what do you think vanilla is extracted into? Sniff some if you're not sure.

Feel free to experiment with wine in the kitchen. Especially if there's someone else around to wash all the dishes. W.C. Fields understood the concept. "I love to cook with wine," he said, "Sometimes I even add it to the food."

A MATCH MADE IN HELL
Can the wine and cheese marriage be saved?

THE MEDIA JUST ADORE KNOCKING the stuffing out of wine snobs. Last year they pounced on a study claiming that blindfolded, you couldn't tell red wine from white. This week they're thrilled to inform us that wine and cheese, that staple of gallery openings everywhere, don't really go together.

"Cheese Spoils Fine Wines—So Stick to the Plonk!" screams one headline. "Wine and Cheese Incompatible," squeals another. And, "Cheese and Wine in Worst Possible Taste."

A study by Hildegarde Heymann, professor of viticulture and enology at the University of California, had 11 trained tasters evaluate a variety of red wines with cheeses ranging from mild to stinky. They concluded that, across the board, cheese mutes flavors and aromas in wine, canceling out oak, berries and tannins.

This is not news to the wine world, where it's common knowledge that cheese and wine make argumentative bed-fellows. Blue cheese, for instance, brings out the bitterness in reds. But the muting effect is not all bad. You might lose fruit, but you also lose excess astringency. For centuries, the wine merchant, like a film director smearing Vaseline on his lens for the aging star's close-up, has obeyed the adage: "Buy over fruit, sell over cheese." If the cheddar cube on a toothpick mellows that plastic glass of red from a box, everyone's happy.

All food changes your perception of wine, which is why technical wine tasters avoid all but a puff of white bread to scour out the mouth. Professional food tasting is as sterile and ritual-prone as wine. While the headlines gleefully crow about "Exploding the myth that a fine cheese can be enhanced by a perfect wine," and "No magical wine and cheese pairing," the study doesn't compare *all the possible things* you could eat with wine. While not perfect, cheese could still be the best.

As foods go, cheese probably comes closest to wine in complexity and variety. Both are about balancing nature with chemical changes and aging. Artisanal cheeses, like wine, are prized for their unique character. You want consistency? Eat Velveeta.

Never mind. The press is too busy gloating. Gotcha! We exposed you, you snob! You don't even know what you're tasting!

Ironically, science also tells us that even if a snob could not pick his $100 bottle out of a lineup it wouldn't matter. If mystique and price make the wine more attractive, it will taste better to him.

Then there's this subhead: "The classic wine and cheese party should become a thing of the past, if U.S. research to be believed."

Let me get this straight: We're going to stop eating something we like because a study informs us we don't really like it? I've always been a little baffled by the idea of "proper" wine and food pairing, anyway. Sure, certain chemicals cancel each other out and chefs match wines to food the way they choose a certain spice or sauce. But "proper," at best, is only a guess at what might taste good to you.

Seven years before she died, my mother met the man of her dreams. Their life together was a whirl of romantic weekends involving black lace undies, chocolate-dipped strawberries and Champagne. Had a lab technician appeared to point out that, scientifically speaking, Champagne does not work with chocolate and strawberries, the happy couple would have been too busy locking lips to bother strangling him with his own stethoscope.

A reader emailed me, "Early on in my drinking career I thought what goes with what was a bunch of crap. Then I thought, 'What do you put on your hamburger? Mustard, dill pickles, big juicy red onions. Maybe other stuff.' It dawned on me that certain kinds of wine taste better with certain kinds of food. VOILA."

Those who need science to tell them what they like will be encouraged to hear that Heymann has just completed a study involving dipping sauces and white wines. She hopes to receive funding for a red wine and chocolate and a white wine and cheese study this year.

As for the rest of you, next time you're perplexed about

pairing wine and food, just shut your eyes, take a few calming breaths and listen to your intuition. You came preprogrammed with this data. You don't need the service patch.

PUNCH, DRUNK
Remember sangria?

YOU MAY HAVE DISCOVERED that one of the downsides to being a grape-nut is that you're expected to bring the wine to potluck dinners and family gatherings. They present the idea like they're doing you a favor. After all, you'd surely turn your nose up at the rinky-dink junk they'd dredge up, in their ignorance. And they rely on your mastery of the food-and-wine match, something they might botch completely. Then they throw in a little flattery, suggesting an audience eager to hear you sound off about your selection. That one's hard to resist. So, as usual, Aunt Helen brings the potato salad and you spring for a case of wine.

Luckily, there's a hot-weather solution that will bust neither your pocketbook nor your wine-savant image: sangria.

Fine for the innocent and cash-strapped, you might think, but what self-respecting wine geek mixes in soda pop and fruit juice? The Spanish, that's who. They don't take wine to be rocket science, and have no problem mixing up this summertime refresher. The Japanese, too, are fond of Mouton-Rothschild 'n Sprite, but that's a different story, and the Mouton is often about as real as street-vendor Ray-Bans.

Take a few deep, cleansing breaths, relax your major muscle groups one at a time, and try to achieve Med: the Mediterranean mindset of olive groves, ripened grain, flopping fish and all things juicy and colorful. Now you're ready.

There are as many sangria recipes as people making it, but the real fun is blending your own. Avoid mixes and bottles of pre-made sangria. You'll do much better with what's ripe at the farmer's market or even just what you've got on hand. Depending on the direction you'd like to see the party take, you can concoct a light thirst-quencher, or a potent, head-spinning cocktail.

Use these four steps as theme, and add your own variations:

1. **Wine:** Start with a full-bodied red. Rioja is the authentic Spanish choice, but New World fruit bombs work beautifully. You can also start with white and make Sangria Blanca. Either way, the wine needn't be great or complex, just decent.

2. **Fruit:** First, citrus fruit, in the form of juice, slices and zest. It balances the sweetness and keeps other fruit from discoloring. Then add any other fruit that tempts you, including peaches, cherries, pears and berries of any kind. Soft things like strawberries should go in just before serving, or they'll turn mushy. Frozen fruit or condensed orange juice and lemonade work, too.

3. **Booze:** Fortify with brandy or an orange liqueur like Cointreau or Grand Marnier. If you like, add sugar to taste. Stir and refrigerate—overnight if possible, but at least two hours.

4. **Fizz:** Now add sparkle in the form of club soda, 7-Up, bitter lemon, or sparkling wine. Then pour into ice-filled glasses and decorate with fresh fruit.

At your next fiesta, instead of wistfully watching your greedy friends drain bottle after bottle of your hard-earned wine, pour sangria with a heavy hand and a light heart. Won't you be the sport.

Here's a recipe to get you started:

Combine:
2 bottles full-bodied red wine
$1/2$ cup orange liqueur
1 orange, 1 lemon and 1 lime, sliced and muddled with
$1/2$ cup sugar

Refrigerate overnight. Before serving, add 2 bottles chilled sparkling water, pour over ice and garnish with mint and fresh fruit. Olé.

MULL ON THIS
Glögg, gluwein and other comforts

TO A SIX-YEAR-OLD, dads are an identifiable species. They have deep voices, wear ties and go to work carrying a briefcase. Except for mine. Instead of a tie he wore a motorcycle helmet. He never went anywhere near work, and what he carried was a bottle of glug. That was his name for the brown glass bottle of elixir of turpen-hydrate and codeine which went everywhere with him.

It required no prescription in those days, still, it was somewhat controlled. So much of our father-daughter bonding was spent making the rounds of local pharmacies to put by the week's supply of glug. Once or twice I took a surreptitious swig —it tasted like pins and needles.

My first grade sewing project was a custom glug-bottle holder made of red felt and, my father liked to remind me, a lot of left over pins. The drug angle didn't seem to faze my teacher at the time, but that was long before social services stuck their long nose under the family tent.

Glug was his comfort. We all have ours. The real glügg, or glög or gluwein or even vin brulée in the north of Italy, brings solace to many during long winters. The further north you get, the more elaborate and specific the rituals and recipes.

Since the dawn of wine, it's been infused with herbs and spices. Mostly because so much of it was undrinkable without doctoring. But even now that good, inexpensive wine is available everywhere, there's nothing like the comfort of a warm mug, steaming with cinnamon, cloves and orange peel.

Despite a variety of recipes and theories, all have a few things in common, and are adaptable to pretty much anything you have on hand, which in my case can be pretty slim pickings. The basic principles:

Wine: Should be fruit-centered and not too tannic. Nothing great or complex, but at least something you'd drink.

Sugar: Masks excess tannin and acidity.

Citrus: Keeps sugar lively and the potion from cloying.

Spice: Adds aromas, the sort that beckon you down from the slopes and into the lodge. Especially warm, pumpkin pie, Christmas spices, like cinnamon, cardamom, cloves and nutmeg. Wrap them in cheese cloth and steep like a teabag to avoid straining. Keep a premix on hand. Or leave spices in unflavored schnapps for a few days and then use this infusion to prepare your glug.

Spirit: A dash of brandy, rum or other booze add body and kick. Other traditional ingredients include herbal or citrus tea, cream, ground almonds, and even stranger things.

Heat: Some old cookbooks advocate boiling the wine for ten minutes, which evaporates the alcohol. I think that defeats the purpose. Better to heat to just before the boiling point. A Crockpot is perfect. It heats slowly and you can keep adding ingredients as your crowd of friends ebbs and flows.

Steep and Strain: After simmering a while, put it all through a strainer and serve. Or steep mixture overnight in the fridge, to let flavors integrate, then strain and reheat before serving.

Strange but True: Swedes also add raisins which swell up and get very potent. Guests fish them out of their mugs with spoons, then drain them against the side of the cup, scoop onto spicy gingerbread cookies and eat like little open faced sandwiches.

The recipes below are only jumping-off points. Use what's on hand, feel free to experiment and remember, it's almost impossible to go wrong. When in doubt, add more sugar or honey.

Finally, if you're too lazy or self-centered for these methods, it's time for Micro-Mull. Fill a mug three-quarters of the way with red wine, add spices, sugar, a little brandy, Cointreau or amaretto, and microwave on high for one minute. Remove, stir well, and drink, filtering the spices through your teeth like a baleen whale. And be sure to put your feet up by a roaring fire. Glug glug!

Classic Mulled Red Wine
1 bottle fruity, lower tannin red wine like Syrah,
Zinfandel or Merlot
1 orange
1 lemon
2 cardomom pods
6 whole cloves
6 whole black peppercorns
2 cinnamon sticks, plus 4 for garnish
1/2 cup brown sugar
1/2 cup brandy
Crush cardamom pods with flat side of knife. Slice orange and lemon. Combine everything in large pot (not aluminum). Cook over medium heat, stirring until sugar dissolves, 1-2 minutes. Reduce hear to low. Simmer about 30 minutes. Pour through fine mesh sieve to serve. (Or refrigerate overnight first.) Garnish each glass with cinnamon stick and, if you like, a candy cane.

Elizabethan Hippocras
2 1/2 cups white wine (I used an Italian Chardonnay, but anything without too much acid, such as Viognier would work)
1 cup water
8 oz finely ground almonds
1/2 cup white or raw sugar
1/2 tsp ground ginger.
1/2 tsp almond extract.
Put all ingredients in saucepan and simmer, stirring occasionally, for 10 minutes. Can be served hot or cold.

DOES THIS WINE MAKE ME LOOK FAT?
Drink wine, stay skinny

AS IF LOSING WEIGHT WEREN'T HARD ENOUGH, most diets insist you do it in wine-less misery. For centuries before the birth of the bacon cheeseburger, though, we drank wine and we were thin. Could we be scaping the wrong goat?

It doesn't take a marathon to work off the 80 to 120 calories in a four-ounce glass of red or white. But shouldn't you avoid these "empty calories" when every bite counts? Actually, as we're finally discovering a few generations after prohibition erased all positive references to alcohol from the medical books, wine is a powerhouse of polyphenols, resveratrol, antioxidants and other goodies that keep cancer, stroke and heart-disease at bay. Hardly an empty pleasure. Besides, moderate wine drinkers (two to three glasses a day, depending on size and gender) get only about 6 percent of their calories from wine, leaving a whopping 94 percent for other nutrients.

Wines labeled "Low-Carb," speeding their way to a store near you, should gladden the hearts of Atkins, Zone and South Beach disciples, at least the ones who weren't aware that *all* dry wine is low-carb. The sugar is fermented into ethanol, which is neither protein, carb nor fat. Wine is a no-no in the Atkins jump-start phase only because it breaks down in your liver *before* you start burning fat, thus delaying the race towards slimness.

Numerous new studies support the enophile who would be thin. Among their findings: Daily wine correlates with lower body mass than occasional drinking does. Moderate wine drinkers have narrower waists and less tummy fat than beer and spirit drinkers and abstainers, even when they consume the same amount of alcohol calories.

Time and again, adding wine to a controlled diet netted no weight gain, and sometimes a loss. Wine drinkers lost more than control groups who drank juice and even water. Among obese patients tracked for a year after stomach-banding surgery, the moderate wine drinkers lost more weight than abstainers.

Women who pop a cork with dinner are half as likely to be obese as non-drinkers. They appear to metabolize alcohol differently from men. But what, exactly, they do with those calories has scientists a bit baffled. Either the wine calories don't fully count somehow, or they promote energy wastage, since study after study shows less weight gain than predicted for calories consumed. One explanation comes from Spain, where scientists found that antioxidants and flavanoids in wine speed the breakdown of fat.

Wine drinkers also eat better, exercise more, and smoke less than other drinkers and abstainers. (Although in that particular study, it's not clear whether they make healthier choices or just know how to sound that way on a survey.)

"Maybe, so," say the diet tsars, "but still—No Wine For You! It's too relaxing. It strips away your dieter's resolve." Indeed, wine can bestow appetite on the sick and anorexic. Paradoxically, it can also provide enough satisfaction to enable you to limit your food intake. In other words, a stalk of celery doesn't look so lonely next to a glass of Riesling.

"But...it's dangerous!" the diet books sputter. "An intoxicating beverage on a dieter's empty stomach!" Listen, if your diet is that severe, you won't stick with it for long. Crash diets are famous for not working. If crash you must, by all means cut out everything but seaweed and sausage casings. But if it's a gradual, enduring lifestyle change you're after, there's a place at the table for wine.

A leitmotif in the diet œuvre is "Slow down, turn off the TV, chew like a chipmunk and pay attention to your food." What better than a glass of wine to make dinner an occasion worth lingering over?

Low-fat, low-carb, Stone Age or Mediterranean, the diet that works best is the one you can live with. Snarfers of Snackwells and Carb-Buster bars are not following doctors' orders. They're obeying the exigencies of the omnipotent god of pleasure and cravings. What you put in your mouth is the most personal of decisions, but it's nice to know that putting wine there probably won't make you fat.

FOOD FIGHT
Board that smorgas!

A CHARDONNAY FROM AUSTRALIA called Swaying Willow bills itself as "The First Diet Wine," with only one-third the usual calories. It promises the "creamy, peachy character you'd expect from a Chardonnay, with a hint of oak on the palate."

The sophisticates of the wine world sneer. And I find that appalling. As a lone wine lover who is not also a gourmand, I find myself wondering: Do you have to choose between gourmet and aesthete? If you love wine, do you also have to love food that is architectural, delicious and deadly? It seems like everywhere fine wine is served, the food is oozing with butter, crème fraîche, and foie gras. And, oh, the ridicule if you don't eat that stuff!

It's not that I don't appreciate flavor, artistry and luscious mouth-feel. I also appreciate the rush of morphine, and the thrill of doing 110 on the highway at night, but I know the consequences, so I refrain.

The gourmet crowd, though, wants to take me down, and they have an arsenal of tactics:

Scorn: "If you're not going to use pure Guernsey, full-fat butter on your bread, you might as well eat it plain. I mean, if you can't believe it's not butter, it's probably cow pee." (Imagine the same person saying, "If you're not going to drive a Ferrari, you might as well walk." Some of us are just…um…differently-budgeted.)

Enabling: "Oh don't worry, that's not clarified butter in the escargot, it's only olive oil." Like a cup of olive oil needs a GPS to find my hips. Shades of the druggie who eases his stigma by getting his friends hooked, too.

Justification cloaked as moral superiority: "In this narcissistic age everyone is obsessed with sweating and eating sprouts. I say, 'to hell with the food police!' " You see, it's not that they don't have the discipline to eat healthy food; they're *above* the concept.

OK, I admit it. I'm vain. But that's only part of it. I want my legs to pump, my arms to swing, my kidneys to filter, and my blood to rush through my veins as long as I live. I wouldn't dream of ruining my car by filling the tank with diesel just because it smelled nice. But if I were that stupid, I could get a new car. Last time I checked, this is the only body I get. And I enjoy it, every bit as much as the foodies enjoy their duck confit.

People who can afford to pay the prices this sort of food commands tend to be responsible types with good credit ratings. They plan their future, pay their bills on time and put money in a 401(k). Yet they cheerfully clog up their personal pipes, saying, "Some day they'll make a pill, and I won't have to worry about all this health stuff." Perhaps, and it may keep them alive, but they'll be missing the joy of piloting a well-working body through space. If you've forgotten that feeling, watch a four-year-old on a swing, head back, eyes shut, hair streaming. The ephemeral bliss of a hazelnut truffle melting on the tongue is a poor tradeoff.

But one I long for sometimes. Does that mean I must choose all or nothing? Does eating (gasp!) fat-free cheese mean my palate failed Shop? And is there something wrong with people who want to drink wine, but choose the diet kind? Are they lesser beings who should content themselves with 7UP if they can't behave properly? If you think so, step outside for a moment and I'll punch your squishy tushy into next week. And, please, at the next winemaker's dinner, couldn't you for once serve, say, some whole grains?

Part 11

Science Projects

JUST WHEN YOU'RE GETTING COMFY with wine, it betrays you. It spills on your carpet. It gives you a migraine, or worse, a hangover. Be prepared with solutions for those calamities. Plus this section also includes some other cool things to do with wine. No, not enemas. That's a different book.

TALES FROM THE DARK SIDE
Hangover helpers

AH, SPRING! Birds cheep merrily, whilst blossoms float lightly to the ground. The days grow longer and a girl's fancy turns to....getting rid of this hangover. Someone ought to glue the damn blossoms back on the branches and stop that infernal racket. Full fathom five my breakfast lies. Oh, yes, we, in the business, also succumb. The difference is we call it research.

In that spirit, I'll tell you what I've learned, so perhaps you will do as I say, not as I spew. Google "Hangover," and you get 364,000 entries. Everyone and his security advisor has a hangover cure. The following information, therefore, is the truth, and nothing but the truth, but it is not the whole truth.

Geometrically speaking, in the axis of evil, dehydration is the hypotenuse. Having your brain shrink from lack of water is not a pretty feeling. The first defense against a hangover is to drink buckets—not glasses—of water, before, during and after the evening in question.

Afraid water will dilute the buzz? It won't. The feel-good part is when your blood-alcohol level is on the rise, and begins to smother your frontal lobes, freeing you up to have fun and sing karaoke. When it's risen, that's all the better you're going to feel. Water chasers actually prolong the process.

But you didn't listen, did you? Now you're waiting for your bed to come to a halt so you can board. Not so fast. When you sleep, your metabolism slows down and takes longer to clear out your system. Each hour you stay awake is an investment in the next morning. While you're up, take some ibuprofen or aspirin—never Tylenol: combining it with booze can damage your liver. If your dinner has been stamped "return to sender," accept delivery. Your nausea will ebb a bit.

Next morning, you awaken weak and light-headed. Alcohol has broken down the sugar stores in your liver. Add Gatorade, or even just a spoonful of sugar to your hydrating plan.

Your slamming headache is probably the work of *congeners*; nasty chemicals up to 30 times more prevalent in dark-colored drinks than light ones. Scotch and Cabernet, for instance, make an ornerier duo than gin and Pinot Gris. Congeners lurk in young, heavily-oaked wines and in cheap plonk. They come in many varieties, each a new hurdle for your overtaxed body. That's why it's wise to nix the mix.

Coffee is a diuretic and irritates your stomach, but it also sooths the headache by constricting blood vessels in the brain. If it's your habit, have at it. You don't want to go through caffeine withdrawal on top of everything else.

You're coming down off of a mild overdose of depressant and your nerves are hypersensitive; in shock. You're malnourished, and did I mention dehydrated? Time to eat. Don't fret over lean-protein and fruit versus milkshake and cheeseburger; just eat anything you can face. Preferably containing tomatoes.

They are your friend. This is half the reason for the Bloody Mary. The other half is the hair-of-the-dog, which relaxes shattered nerves, numbs the pain and ends withdrawal. Alas, it only postpones the inevitable; better to get detoxing over with. B-complex vitamins, C, and cystene will help, too.

At this point I should present you with some recipes involving things like bananas, raw eggs and Worcestershire sauce, but I'd rather not go there just now, if you don't mind. I'd like to report on the efficacy of these, as well as of my collection of guaranteed, miracle hangover pills. Frankly, though, I don't hang over often enough to be much of a lab rat. So I thought I'd hire some 18-year-old boys and a keg, and experiment on them. I'll get back to you with the results. As long as they're here, maybe they could go out and strangle those birds.

RED WINE, WHITE CARPET, BLUE MOOD
Get stains out

SIX WEEKS ON CRUTCHES IS NOT ALL BAD. You develop deltoids like Superman and people feel sorry for you and open doors. The hard part, though, when your hands are your wheels, is carrying things. Scariest of all is transporting a glass of red wine to safety over a gaping no-man's-land of white carpet. If there's a more frightening sight than a dark splash of red spreading across a snowy rug, I don't know what it is. In order to exorcise that chilling image, we at the House of Klutz Test Kitchens went to work to determine the best way to get red out of white.

Our lab equipment consisted of samples of medium-pile, white wool carpet; a large linen tablecloth ripped in pieces; and a bottle of a red we would just as soon not name but that we had no qualms about spilling. Each cleaning method was tested on an immediate wine-spill as well as a spot that had dried for

24 hours. Judging criteria: spot-disappearance and labor involved. Some cleaners that weren't a hundred percent effective are still good to know about in an emergency when nothing else is available. The results:

Home Remedies

1. Any combination of salt, baking soda, cream of tarter, club soda and white wine: Urban legends! These things don't work! Some cause a stunning red-to-pink transformation, but all leave pink or brown stains behind. Forget about them.

2. Detergent and water: Useful for wiping up new spills immediately, but doesn't completely eradicate them and has little effect on old ones.

3. Milk: Put stained fabric in a saucepan and cover with milk. Bring to a boil, remove from heat and rinse when the stain is gone. It works, though obviously impractical on carpet, but it uses a lot of milk and makes a huge mess when you forget about the pan and let the milk boil over. (We like to test these things for you.)

4. Shaving cream: We are nothing if not cool and objective here at the lab, but we found ourselves rooting for shaving cream. It smells great and it's lovely to play with. You spray it on, work it into the spot with your fingers, then use a warm sponge to clean off the excess. We gave it a few extra chances to prove itself. It was good on fabric and OK on carpet, but the final, dried results, alas, are not completely flawless. We tried some shaving gel, too, figuring that you're more likely to have it around, but it turns the carpet green. The lab, however, plans to continue the shaving cream experiments.

Commercial Preparations

1. Avenge stain remover and Resolve Carpet Cleaner: Both require lots of elbow grease and repetition. Stains remain decidedly pink. Don't bother.

2. **Carbona Stain Devils—Fruit & Red Wine:** Must be measured and dissolved in water. On carpet, it dramatically deconstructs red and turns it into…brown. Not bad on old and new fabric stains.
3. **Gonzo's Wine Out:** Decent results on carpet. Drawback: There's only a tiny bit in the bottle and the spray pump is very hard to use. Turns fabric blue.

And the Winner is
Peroxide & Dawn: A freshly-mixed solution of two parts hydrogen peroxide to one part blue Dawn dishwashing detergent. If you ever drink red wine, write down this formula. It's unbelievable. Pour a little on a spot, rub lightly, sponge off. It left the rug so clean we couldn't even find the spot the next day. Impressive on fabric—not just new or day-old stains, but ancient, many-times-washed ones, too. It's easy, and you probably have the ingredients on hand. If not, stock up immediately and you'll never fear red wine again.

Best runners-up in a pinch: Milk for fabric, shaving cream for carpet. Give the shaving cream a chance. It's almost as much fun as wine.

RED ALERT
Tame the red wine headache

JUDGING BY MY E-MAIL, an alarming number of you have quit drinking red wine because it gives you a headache. Do not go gentle into that good night! As inventions go, red wine ranks right up there with indoor plumbing, Novocaine and the wheel. More than a great pleasure, it's been shown to prevent heart disease, osteoporosis, cancer, memory loss and memory loss. (Note to self: Drink more red wine.)

I'll bet people nag you, "Oh, come on, try a little, you're

just being hypersensitive!" At last, you are vindicated, because now your condition has an official name. If you're one of those folks who gets a pounding headache, perhaps with nausea and flushing, within an hour or less of drinking even a small glass of red wine, you have Red Wine Headache Syndrome.

Since RWHS research has nothing to do with weight loss or baldness, and it's not sexually transmitted, it doesn't get much press. But, rest assured, scientists are working hard on your problem, and the latest studies conclude…that they haven't the slightest idea what's going on. Which is a big improvement over when they thought they knew, and were wrong. But there is still hope for you. Let's start by busting a few myths.

First, the culprit is *not* sulfites. All wine contains sulfites, or SO_2. For thousands of years, winemakers have welcomed its stabilizing effect, adding it at crucial intervals during vinification. Only American labels require the ominous warning, "Contains Sulfites," if the level exceeds ten parts per million. This happens to be about the level you get if you don't add any, since SO_2 is a natural presence on grape skins. That's why another label you might have seen, "No Sulfites Added," is a bit disingenuous. However, the point is moot anyway, unless you are one of the very few, severely steroid-dependent asthmatics who actually is sulfite-sensitive. If so, you react much more violently to dried fruit, hot dogs and many other processed foods, because they have thousands of times the SO_2 found in wine.

Second, it's probably not the histamines, unless your headache comes with itching, sneezing, shortness of breath and diarrhea. If so, red is indeed the enemy, since the devil is in the skins, which give red its color. Good news! Taking an antihistamine before drinking should prevent the reaction. Just make sure to choose a non-drowsy formula if you want to remember the evening instead of being remembered as the one who slid under the table.

The latest theory is that RWHS is caused by prostaglandin, which certain people lack the wherewithal to metabolize. Scientists admit that it might be caused by yet another substance, probably something in the strains of yeast or bacteria found in red wine. But they vow to soldier on until they've cornered the enemy, despite the obvious strain of having to drink all that leftover red wine in the lab.

But, more good news! Former sufferers are getting results from prostaglandin-inhibitors, namely ibuprofen and Nuprin, as well as the weaker, but workable, aspirin. Take them less than an hour before drinking and chances are no headache will develop. If you should wake up the next morning with a headache, what you've got is known as "a hangover," a medical condition that definitely deserves more research.

Best bet is to test this preventative with just a few sips of wine. And since I'm not a doctor (although I play one in the bedroom with my boyfriend), you should certainly consult your MD first.

So, now you, too, can be a wine snob, with your very own Wine Syndrome! When the conversation turns to MLF or carbonic maceration, try tossing in, "I find the aggressive delivery of RWH in this Volnay surprisingly muted by the prosto-inhibitors, don't you?" Then smile mysteriously and enjoy, at long last, your red.

DOMAINE LE GARAGE
Make wine at home

MANY PEOPLE OF A CERTAIN AGE, upon finding I write about wine, tell me that their first sip came from grandfather's homemade barrels in the cellar. During the long winter months when most other agricultural pursuits are out of the question, you, too, could be making memories for your children, by taking up the hobby of making your own wine.

It involves surprisingly little space or equipment, and besides being fun and satisfying, will give you a much better understanding of what wineries go through to bring you their product. Once you taste the fruit of your own labors, you will have a new appreciation for wine you once sneered at from the liquor store. Properly executed, even your first efforts should be drinkable, and, with practice, you can make some fairly decent stuff in your own basement.

You'll need more detailed instructions if you decide to pursue it, but here's a thumbnail sketch of what's involved:

First, the grapes. Though a romantic vision of barefoot grape-stomping festivals may cross your mind, don't go there. As a beginner, you're much better off buying vinifera (as opposed to Welch's) grape juice, suitable for fermenting and available at the winemaking stores where you'll be buying your other supplies. You can choose from Cabernet, Merlot, Chardonnay and others, and you don't have to mess with stems, skins and grape shipments.

Next you need yeast, and a couple of five-gallon, glass carboys. You'll add yeast to your juice, stand back, and watch it ferment. It will foam and sizzle, and look disgusting for about five days, during which you occasionally stir it. You have to be careful at this stage, because once you see what yeast can do to sugar, you're going to want to try fermenting everything you can get your hands on, from peaches to asparagus. Try not to get sidetracked.

Fermentation kills off unwanted bacteria, but once it's finished you must prevent contamination from ruining the wine. You'll be doing a lot of disinfecting, as well as measuring sugar and chemicals, which will make you feel like a mad scientist, but hopefully you won't blow anything up. When the wine is fermented you rack it into a clean container. This is accomplished by putting the carboy of wine on something higher, such as the sink, putting an empty carboy on something lower, such as the bathtub, and, by means of a plastic hose, siphoning wine from one to the other. You'll do this again later to clear the wine, leaving the sediment, or *lees*, behind.

Now comes the boring part. The wine has to age for a few months, until the carbonation and roughness are gone. This is a good time to design your labels. There's even software available for this, so you won't tax your creativity too much. It's a good idea to put the variety and year on them, as well as the name and a picture of your personal château, such as "Apartment 31B Zinfandel, Vintage 2006."

Eventually, it will be time to bottle. Use a funnel, and fill the remaining headspace with nitrogen or carbon dioxide, so there's no room for destructive oxygen. While you're at this, your corks are soaking to make them pliable. You'll need to rent or borrow a corking machine, employed with a slot-machine gesture to compress corks and stuff them in.

Then, slap on your labels, lay the bottles down in a cool dark place and allow them to rest past the "bottle sickness" phase, a transition that occurs with all wines.

After this, it's merely a matter of pulling out a bottle to impress the kinfolk and afford you the satisfaction of knowing that you spent $15 a bottle to make something that would have cost you about $5.29 in a store. But doesn't it feel good!

MOTHER, MAY I?
Turn leftovers into vinegar

WHO DO I THINK I AM, passing judgment on wine? It's not like I can make it myself. My one effort, many moons ago, proudly vinified and bottled in my bathroom (using the sink-to-toilet-to-tub altitude ratio, an important element in the gravity-fed, racking process) elicited this comment from my mother:

"Stop sending me that awful stuff!"

The fact that she said the same thing about my writing might explain my ambivalent reaction to Mother, the frightening blob of protoplasm that spins wine into vinegar. A valuable commodity, it's been lovingly nursed and divided among vinegaristas since the day it crawled out of the primordial swamp and into a salad.

I don't like living alone with it. But I also don't like pouring good wine down the sink when there aren't enough neighbors to handle all the bottles I open and taste. So I started making vinegar.

Like winemaking, the pace is slow. As hobbies go, bonsai probably gives more instant gratification. But, unlike winemaking, it's hard to screw up. If you take all the recipes and toss out the parts where they contradict one another (add water; don't, only red; only white…) it boils down to this: Pour your leftover wine into an open-topped container, add Mother, and wait. After about three months, voila! It's vinegar and you can start using it. It will be pretty harsh, though, so you might want to draw some off to filter and age—on oak chips if you're feeling frisky. Meanwhile, you keep adding leftovers to the mother ship…indefinitely.

I'm pretty proud of my little factory, or at least I was until I visited an *acetaia* in Italy and saw what it took to put the balls in balsamic, that dark, dense, bitter-sweet elixir that's more at home on a scoop of ice-cream than in salad dressing.

It starts as white juice from the Trebbiano grape, boiled down to a sugary concentrate. After fermenting, it moves to the *batteria*: a row of barrels descending in size from about ten gallons to two. Unlike the dank cellar of a winery, this barrel room is surprisingly hot—the better to thicken the vinegar. But all that evaporation leaves air-space in the barrels. So, once a year, they top up the smallest barrel with juice from the one next to it. That one, in turn, is filled from its neighbor and so on up to the biggest barrel, which is topped up with new must. If you know sherry, you'll recognize a *solera*.

Each barrel is a different wood. Over the course of 12 to 50 years aging, balsamic picks up a rainbow of flavors from ash and cherry, juniper and oak. Every year a tiny amount is tapped and bottled from the baby barrel. All that time and work add up to a serious price. Balsamic that costs less than a comparable amount of grand cru Bordeaux could not possibly be the real thing. The Modena region has dibs on the word balsamic, but other areas of Italy use this system and label it *tradizionale*.

Don't let this flight into the sublime discourage you from your own adventures with vinegar making. What have you got to lose? The worst that can happen is you end up with Nuit St. Georges Tub and Tile cleaner.

You might also find that turning your excess wine into something useful soothes your conscience in an illogical but comforting way, just as resolving the paper-or-plastic perplex does for some people. You can then bottle it, label it and give it to all your friends at Christmas, so *they* can pour it down the sink. Be sure to send some to your mother.

Appendixes

Here is the official "reference" section, which you should occasionally "thumb through" with your "thumbs." You'll find crucial facts, like how to get drunk in any country in the world. Plus, the true meaning of *Staatliche Weinbaudomane Schloss Bockelheimer Kupfergrube Kabinett Nahe.* And how everything you know about wine is wrong. I also included useful things like a questionnaire (Fill it out together! In bed!) and some extra "quotation marks."

ENCYCLOPEDIA OF WINE HOKUM
or
NEW STUDIES ON OLD HOGWASH
Everything you know that's true, ain't

(Being a Compendium of Delusion, Fallacy, Ignus Fatuus, Erratum and Terminological Inexactitude)

Enough myths about wine persist to fill an encyclopedia. This short one, anyway. Sommeliers, producers, drinkers and, yup, even wine writers cling to notions that simply ain't true—not surprising in a field that changes as fast as a lunch-hour shopper at Loehmann's. Herewith: a short guide to wine lies that just won't die.

Age: A necessity back when young wine had the softness of Brillo and the finish of Drano. Nowadays, most wine comes ready to drink and doesn't get any better. A few can still go the distance, but they're not for everyone. The bottle giveth complexity, but taketh away fruit.

Big: We Americans like our wine purple as ink, reeking of oak and concentrated as a Russian chess champion. Amps turned up, we're easily underwhelmed by the un-plugged elegance of Old World wine. Turn that sucker down to discover a whole new type of dinner music.

Blend: You put milk in your coffee, sugar in your tea, but you wouldn't dream of doctoring wine. Why not? It's fun to experiment! Add a drop of lemon juice, or a pinch of sugar. Pour a little Merlot in your Cab. You'll learn a lot, and I promise the winemaker isn't looking.

Box: Chardonnay-flavored apple juice trashed its reputation, but actually a very useful container and perfectly respectable to Brits and Aussies. Light and stackable, its vacuum-bag/faucet combo keeps wine fresh for weeks after tapping. Good wines, cubed, should be available very soon. Stay tuned.

Breathing: Opened bottles do as much of this as you would locked in the trunk of a Buick with a straw. If your wine wants air—and many do—pour it into a glass, pitcher or decanter. In emergency situations, consider mouth-to-mouth.

Burgundy: The jug years left us thinking it was purple and hearty, when in fact real Burgundy is none other than Pinot Noir—more brains than brawn, and more brown than purple. What does that leave for your hearty beef stew? Zinfandel! It's the new Burgundy.

Cans: First a box, and now—a six-pack? You want Freedom Fries with that? Actually, nothing stands between cans and the wine market but their image. Take a four-pack of Aussie Wine's surprisingly decent Shiraz on your next picnic and you can skip the attitude as well as the corkscrew.

Chianti Classico: Sounds like a classier level of Chianti, but actually a sub-region of Chianti, the way that bald spot is a sub-region of your head, except in this case it's considered prime real estate.

Clarity: Save it for diamonds. Clear means filtered, thus safe from spoilage. The pros and cons of pasteurized cheese apply here: Filtering removes unwanted microbes and yeast, but also flavors. Good wine can range from brilliant to downright hazy these days, the only drawback to the latter being you can't magnify the menu through your Muscat when you forget your reading glasses.

Cork: State-of-the-art stopper for 250 years, unfortunately also a spongy condo for mold and bacteria. Cork has now been replaced with more reliable, hygienic closures. At least in the case of poison, medicine and food. Wine, however, still clings to these pieces of tree bark—chiefly because they go "pop!"

Expensive: What great wine is, right? An orangutan can order good $500 wine. OK, an orangutan with plastic and a decent French accent. But plenty of cheaper wines are swell, too. Land, labor and marketing costs are a few of the factors that goose up price but not flavor. Complexity costs, but if you'd rather quaff than analyze, it's a waste of dough. The best wine is the star in your price bracket—whether that's $6, $16 or $50.

Fattening: Diet-guru/sadists notwithstanding, there's no evidence that wine makes you fat and plenty to the contrary. Zero fat, zero carbohydrates (when sugar turns to alcohol the carbs are lost), takes half a bottle to equal the calories in one Snicker's bar. In a recent study, obese patients, particularly women, who added wine to their diet lost more weight than a control group. Does it replace nutrition? Moderate drinkers get about 6 percent of their energy from wine which means they derive 94 percent from other sources. Does it weaken dieters' resolve? You might argue that facing steamed chicken and broccoli every night would be unbearable without it.

German: No longer limited to sweet, sweeter and Blue Nun-of-the-above, delicious German Riesling is one of the world's great bargains. Often bone-dry, it's fabulous with food and low in alcohol so you get to drink more. If only the bottle would fit in your fridge.

Headache: Quit blaming sulfites. Cheese, hot dogs and dried fruit have lots more of them. The real culprit is still on the loose, but probably lurks in the skins, a much bigger factor in red wine than white. If Euro-wines are kinder on your skull, it's probably due to the thinner-skinned grapes their climates produce.

Kabinett: Not a guarantee of dryness, only of grape-sugar level at harvest, like you care. Trocken means dry, but you can't always trust it. Either get to know your German regions, or ask someone who's tasted the wine. I said it was out there, I didn't say it was easy.

Kosher: Kiddush Kool-Aid no longer, today's kosher wine is not your father's Manischewitz (unless he paid for it). Chardonnay, Cabernet, Merlot—kosher now runs the flavor and quality gamut. Why is this wine different from all other wines? It's made only from Sunday through Friday in special equipment with a guy in a beanie supervising.

Legs: Those "tears" running down the side of your glass are are thick and slow when wine is high in alcohol or sugar, and thin and fast if not. But, unlike Queen Anne chairs and sumo wrestlers, wine cannot be said to have "nice legs."

Magnets: Whether embedded in a coaster, clipped around the bottle's neck or plugged in with lights zapping, magnets neither align molecules, rearrange tannins, restructure acids nor do anything else to instantly age or mellow wine. If you experiment with their effects long enough, however, you might find yourself horizontally aligned with Earth's magnetic field.

Meritage: Faux-French impresses some people but not the Meritage Association. Members use the term to ID their Bordeaux blend—outsiders with different blends may not. When a sommelier asks if you'd like the "merit-tahj," why not demonstrate how the offspring of "merit" and "heritage" should be pronounced?

Organic: Still contains sulfites, a natural part of every wine. Organic winemaking is a tricky proposal, with unstable, sometimes weird results. Organic grape farming, however, is both hip and respectable and produces some of the world's great wines.

Punt: The dent in the bottom of the bottle does not correlate with quality. It does, however, cut into wine-space, requiring a bigger bottle, so it looks like you're getting more. Perhaps companies who pull this off are smart enough to make better wine, too.

Red: The required color for important wine, according to certain connoisseurs, who want no truck with Alsatian Riesling, white Burgundy, Hungarian Tokaj, German Eiswein and a rainbow of other goodies. It's their loss and leaves more wine for the rest of us.

Reserve: In some countries, a regulated statement about how long wine has been aged, barreled, or artfully strewn with cobwebs. In America, carries the legal punch of "Farm-Fresh" or "Going-out-of-Business!!!" Some producers save it for their best batches while others slap it on their cheapest junk to give it an aura of class.

Room temperature: Right idea, wrong room, unless your commute home involves spelunking. Flavors go flat and alcohol burns if red wine is served much over 65°F, the ambient temperature of a damp château. In most states they will not shoot you if you ask for an ice bucket for red.

Rosé: Not just for girls and metrosexuals. Good rosé is bone-dry and wonderful on a hot day. If your inner Cro-Magnon still cringes at the color, think of it as salmon or copper. Red with its shirt off. Beer without the belly.

Screwcap: Ripple's Revenge will be the seal of the future, dooming corks to the dustbins of history and the cellars of gamblers. Do not be alarmed at the unarmed sommelier. Shudder only at the prospect of buying wine for long-term aging in any other sort of top.

Silver spoon: Drop one in the neck of an opened Champagne bottle and you'll have bubbles to spare tomorrow. Skip the spoon and you'll still have bubbles. It's the fridge that keeps them in solution. At least in theory. To date, no one has ever succeeded in completing an experiment that requires not finishing a bottle of Champagne.

Stains: When Syrah spills, forget the salt and white wine, both failures in recent tests to remove red wine from silk, cotton, nylon and wool. Hydrogen peroxide mixed with liquid dish soap was a winner, as was a product called Wine Away, developed to get blood off of surgeon's gowns, a plus when the owner of the carpet sees what you've done.

Storage: Scrolly, wrought-iron holders notwithstanding, countertops are a lousy place to keep wine. Ditto those built-in racks over stove and fridge, so beloved by kitchen designers. When you put away wine, think damp, cool, quiet and dark, like the mother-in-law apartment you'd build if your spouse's mom were Dracula. Oh wait, she is.

Sulfites: Present in all wine, but only America requires a warning on the label. Nature's preservatives, they occur naturally in all wine, but sometimes—OK, often—need a little boost. Only adverse effect: The resulting better wine is a drain on the beer industry.

Sweet: Not just for beginners, even though most people start with sweet, pink, fizz (which, incidentally, describes virtually all wine up until the last 200 years, and is still the preferred flavor profile for most of mankind). World-class wines from off-dry to "bellybutton" super-stickies prove that sophisticated and yummy are not mutually exclusive.

Syrah, Petite Sirah, Shiraz: Which one doesn't belong? One and three are French and Aussie names for the same grape. Petite Sirah is whole 'nother beast, a stealth grape that uses its sound-alike name to glom glory from the other two. Once just a blender, it's now featured solo, but still up to its deceptive tricks: One taste will tell you it's anything but petite.

Tongue map: Vee haf vays to make you taste. The familiar diagram showing sweet receptors at the tip, bitter in back and so on is a mistranslation of an early-1900s German thesis, now disproven. Taste buds are multi-taskers, varying from person to person and sprawling, most un-Germanically, past your tongue into your throat and even the roof of your mouth.

Tastevin: The ashtray-on-a-chain that elevates sommeliers above mere mortals long outlived any practical purpose. The days when merchants needed its silver facets to reflect scant, flickering, candlelight into the wine they were buying are over. So if your som uses his to taste, you have my permission to snicker.

Varietal: Adjective, often referring to wine made from and named for a single grape. Thus a bottle labeled "Chardonnay" is described as *varietal* but the grape it's made from is a *variety*. (Note: for betting purposes only. Do not deploy in social settings unless you're already so annoying you have no friends left to alienate.)

Vinho Verde: Red and white and green all over. Called green (verde) because it's picked young, this slightly spritzy wine comes both red and white. Since most of the red is polished off at home, only white is exported, leading people to think that the green in its name refers to white. Or something like that.

Zinfandel: You probably already knew that this red grape saved its skin by making white wine that was really pink. You may also know that, considered America's only serious wine grape, it's actually Croatian and closely related to Italy's Primitivo. But I couldn't find another Z to end this encyclopedia, except for Zellenberg, a tiny town in Alsace where the only myth is that you won't care that the hotel room is actually smaller than the bed they cram in there but then in the end the view was so gorgeous that I didn't.

GERMAN JUNGLE
*Everything you always wanted to know about sekts
but were afraid to ask*

German wine is scary. Just try pronouncing it. When I say "Gewürztraminer" people answer "Gesundheit!"

And if you think pronunciation is tough, just try reading the labels. Even if you understand the words you still don't know what they're supposed to mean.

This explanation of German wine labels is not for the faint of heart. Feel free to contact me if you spot an error. German labels are a living, growing organism. By the time you read this there will no doubt be three new layers of regulations. I am fully aware that this is but a drop in the German wine-law bucket, but if I didn't leave some details out—the exact ones that you undoubtedly know—this would take a week to read.

We'll start by dissecting the label below. Then you'll get to practice and test yourself on a few labels. At the end is a pronunciation guide.

1. Grape variety

If one grape makes up 85 percent or more of the wine, it's listed. Examples: Riesling, Gewürztraminer, Müller-Thurgau. If there's no grape name, it's a blend, called whatever the proprietor wants to call it. Examples: "Liebfraumilch" and "Schwarze Katz."

2. Vintage

If 85 percent of the grapes came from one year, the vintage is allowed (but not required) to be listed. It's often followed by -er. Example: 1996er.

3. Region

There are 13 wine regions in Germany. The ones you see most in the U.S. are: Mosel-Saar-Ruwer, Mittelrhein, Rheingau, Nahe, Rheinhessen and Pfalz.

4. Village/vineyard

A two-word statement. Examples: "Piesporter Goldtröpfchen" and "Wehlener Klosterberg." You know it's the village/vineyard statement, because the first word, which is the village, ends in -er. In our example, *Oestrich* is the village, and this wine is a *Oestricher*, the way you might be a New Yorker.

The second word, *Lenchen* on the sample label, is the name of either a single vineyard, or a group of vineyards. A single vineyard is called an **Einzellage** (einzel = singular, lage = site). A small group of contiguous vineyards is called a **Grosslage** (gross = bulk). *Lenchen* is an Einzellage.

Unless you memorize all 3,000 or so named vineyards, and all 160 Grosslagen, there's no way of knowing if you're looking at an Einzellage or a Grosslage, but either way, it's where the grapes were grown, and it comes right after the village.

(The actual words *Einzellage* and *Grosslage* do not appear on the label. They are used here purely to show off.)

There are a few estates or individual vineyards that are so

well known that they're considered *communities,* and don't use an additional town name. They are: *Schloss Vollrads, Schloss Johannisberg, Steinberg,* and *Schloss Reichartshausen* in the Rheingau; and *Josephshofer* and *Scharzhofberger* in Mosel-Saar-Ruwer.

Review

Two words, first one ending in -er = village/vineyard or village/grosslage.

You're doing great! Now we get into the really fun stuff:

5. Quality classification

There are two legal wine-quality levels for all of Europe: Table Wine and Quality Wine. Under each of those categories you find different sub-categories in each country.

In Germany, category name or initial appears on the bottle. They are:

A. <u>Table Wine (Tafelwein)</u>

 1. **Tafelwein (T)** = Grapes can come partly from other countries.

 2. **Deutscher Tafelwein (DT)** = German table wine, with more than 50 percent of the grapes coming from Germany.

 3. **Landwein (L) =** Country wine.

B. <u>Quality Wine (Qualitätswein)</u>

 1. **Qualitätswein bestimmten Anbaugebietes (QbA)** = Quality wine from a specific region.

 2. **Qualitätswein mit Prädikat (QmP)** = Quality wine with distinction.

This last category, the "Prädikat" level, is itself divided into six categories. They're determined by the ripeness of grapes at harvest, which is the same thing as saying the potential alcohol level. You can have different levels within the same vineyard, if you pick some of the grapes earlier, when sugar level is lower, and some of them later, when sugar is higher.

*6. Prädikat level

A. Kabinett: Literally "cabinet," which is where they used to keep the good bottle to bring out for guests. The lightest wine.
B. Spätlese: "Late harvest." Fuller body than Kabinett.
C. Auslese: "Selected late harvest." The ripest bunches are chosen in repeated trips through the vineyard. Even heavier.
D. Beerenauslese (BA): "Selected berries; late harvest." The ripest individual grapes are chosen in repeated trips through the vineyard. Very sweet dessert wine.
E. Eiswein: "Ice wine." Same ripeness requirement as Beerenauslese. The grapes freeze on the vine before picking. Also very sweet, intense dessert wine.
F. Trockenbeerenauslese (TBA): "Individual dried berries, selected late harvest." In this case, the grapes hang so long that they dry up on the vine a little, like wet raisins. They have to be pressed hard to get any juice, and it takes about 20,000 grapes to make a bottle of wine. Both BA and TBA are almost always affected by *botrytis cinerea*, or noble rot. The resulting wine is very sweet, very concentrated and should also have high acid, so it's not cloying.

*Remember: these categories won't appear unless the wine is at the QmP level.

The harvest schedule is very strict. The beginning of the Kabinett harvest starts a "clock" for all five Prädikat levels. Anything picked during the first six days and 23 hours of harvest is considered Kabinett. You cannot start picking Spätlese until seven days, to the hour, after Kabinett picking has begun. You are, however, allowed to pick Auslese *during* Spätlese harvest, because Auslesen are the early, overripe bunches that are selected separately. Depending on grape variety, BA needs

35 to 40 additional days of hang-time and TBA gets twice that. Riesling is a late-ripening grape to begin with, which can push a TBA harvest as late as February. Because the weather is only good enough to do this about once in a decade, Riesling Trockenbeerenauslese is very rare and very expensive, which is a shame, because it's delicious and so much fun to say.

Prädikat levels do not tell you whether the wine is sweet, semi-sweet or dry. The first three, Kabinett, Spätlese and Auslese can fall in any one of those categories.

Sometimes there's a:

*Residual Sugar (RS) Statement
Trocken = dry, or less than 0.9 percent RS
Halbtrocken = half-dry, or less than 1.8 percent RS

*But, as you can see, neither of those words appears on your sample label. So, how can you tell? Alas, you can't. Knowing residual sugar (RS) level doesn't always help, since it doesn't necessarily correlate with how sweet the wine tastes. But because it helps a *little*, at the end of this chapter you'll find a secret RS decoder chart, courtesy of the International Wine Guild.

7. Weingut
An estate that makes and bottles its own wine.

8. Producer
The producer's name is what's left over: *Spreitzer*. I wish there were a more scientific way to identify it, but there isn't. It's sometimes on the top, sometimes in a scrolly ribbon, but not always either. Usually under or near it, but in this case running up the right side of the label, you'll find the:

9. Address

The letter D (for Deutschland), followed by a postal code and then the address of the producer: D-65375 *Oestrich-Winkel*."

Under the Quality Classification is the word *Erzeugerabfüllung*. This is the:

10. Bottling Statement

Not terribly important for most practical purposes, still it's good to know you're not missing something. Here's what they mean:

A. **Aus dem Lesegut:** Bottled by the producer. May be grown by others. Generally used by negociants.

B. **Erzeugerabfüllung:** Bottled by the grower. This could be a co-op with grower members.

C. **Erzeugergemeinschaft:** Produced and bottled by the co-op.

D. **Gutsabfüllung:** Estate bottled. Can only be used by *Weinguten*

E. **Schlossabfüllung:** Château/castle bottled.

11. AP Nr.

Or, *Amtliche Prüfungsnummer*. Found on all QbA and QmP labels. It's a code, indicating the testing station, vineyard code, bottler code and bottling year. In this case, 2 is the testing station, 101 is the village, 006 the code for the winery and 02 the year that samples were submitted for testing.

12. Cool little symbol

The sign of the VDP or Verband Deutscher Prädikatsweingüter (Association of German Predicates), an organization of the top 200 or so producers—voted on by the producers themselves, not the government.

Lucky you! To simplify things, the VDP has just introduced a new quality classification system that has me banging my head against the computer screen. Since they can't change the government classifications listed above, which *must* appear on the label, this new VDP stuff is *in addition* to all that. A very brief summary:

A. Only the top VDP wines put the *vineyard* on their label. This means you've got lousy, *non*-VDP producers *listing* vineyards, and pretty good, but not top, VDP-producers *not* listing vineyards.

B. A three-layer pyramid of classification, from table wine to top wines. If you'd like all the details of this, you've probably lost your marbles, but email and I'll give it to you. For now, we'll just look at the top level.

C. Top level of VDP wines—only 2 percent of German production. Dry wines, Spätlese level or above, get a special name: *Erstes Gewächs* in the Rheingau and *Grosses Gewächs* everywhere else. Except in Mosel-Saar-Ruwer, where top wines, dry or sweet, QbA to Auselese, get the name *Erste Lage*. (I asked the VDP if the quality designations were different in each region. Answer: "No. They're the same all over the country. With regional variations.")

D. Sweet dessert wines: BA, Eiswein and TBA, also belong at this top level, but do not carry one of these catchy names.

13. Other cool little symbol:
VDP is not the only non-government body with its own system. A group of fifty top producers in the Rheingau have come up with their own:

<u>Charta:</u> indicates a dry, high quality wine.

In case all this is too simple, there are a few more systems:

Classic: a dry, Kabinett level wine, correct to type, as they say, although not necessarily of a certain quality.

<u>Selection:</u> same as Classic, but higher quality.

Producers are also reviving an unofficial term:

<u>Feinherb:</u> means whatever the grower wants, but generally a dry-ish wine like halb-trocken, but decided by taste, not sugar measurement.

All that's left on this label is:

Alcohol percentage: 8.0 percent (low alcohol is one of the great things about German wine—you can drink a lot more of it before passing out!)

Bottle size: 750ml.

You did it! Ready to practice on some labels? There are samples on pages 200 and 209. Plus, here's the residual sugar calculator I promised.

Feel free to copy and print it out, laminate it (scotch tape works) and keep it in your wallet. It only applies to Riesling wine, but other grapes are usually similar.

POTENTIAL ALCOHOL - RIESLING				
𝕂	𝕊	𝔄	𝔅𝔄	𝕋𝔅𝔄
Group 1 8.6%	10.0%	11.1%	15.3%	21.5%
Group 2 9.5%	11.4%	13%	17.7%	21.5%
Group 3 9.1%	10.3%	11.4%	16.9%	21.5%
Group 4 9.5%	11.4%	13%	16.9%	21.5%
Group 5	Wines finished dry (trocken)			

Group 1	Ahr, Mosel-Saar-Ruwer, Mittelrhein	𝕂	Kabinet
Group 2	Hessische-Bergstrasse, Rheingau	𝕊	Spätlese
Group 3	Nahe	𝔄	Auslese
Group 4	Rheinhessen, Pfalz, Baden	𝔅𝔄	Beerenauslese
Group 5	Franken, Wurttemberg	𝕋𝔅𝔄	Trokenbeerenauslese

To Calculate Residual Sugar:

(Potential alcohol minus alcohol % on bottle) x 2

< 1 = dry

1- 4 = off dry

> 4 = sweet

Wein auf Bier, das rat' ich dir.
Bier auf Wein, das laß sein.

(Wine after beer, nothing to fear. Beer after wine, that's not so fine.)
~ German advice to drinkers

8. Producer

7. Weingut

9. Address

4. Village/ vineyard

2. Vintage

1. Grape variety

6. Prädikat level

10. Bottling statement

3. Region

5. Quality classification

11. A.P. Nr.

WHEN IN ROME
Make friends everywhere;
how to say "Cheers!" around the globe

(We accept and appreciate corrections and additions from qualified international quaffers. Send to: corkjester@corkjester.com)

Albania
Gëzuar
Armenia
Genatzt, Genatsoot *"Life"*
Austria
Prosit, Prost
Azerbaijan
Afiyæt oslun
Australia
Cheers
Basque Regions
On egin
Belgium
Op uw gezondheid (Flemish)
Brazil
Saude *"To your health,"* Viva, Topa, Tim-tim, Tchim-tchim
Bulgaria
Na zdrave *"To your health"*
China
Nien nien nu, Kong chien, Yung sing *"Drink and win"*
(Cantonese) Gom bui *or* Gan bei *"Dry the cup"*
Costa Rica
Pura Vida *"Pure life"*
Croatia
Živjeli
Czech
Na zdraví *"To your health,"* Nazdar

Egypt
Fee sihetak, Bisochtak
England
Cheers, Cheerio, Let's toast, Here's mud in your eye
Down the hatch (vulgar)
Estonia
Tervist, Teie, Terviseks *"To your health"*
Ethiopia
T'chen chen
ô
Faroe Islands
Skál
Finland
Kippis, Kippis terveydeksi *"To your health"*
Maljanne (more polite), N Malja *"A toast to..."*
Pohjanmaan kautta *"By way of Ostrobothnia"* (historical reference)
Hölkyn kölkyn *(doesn't mean anything but sounds funny)*
France
À vôtre santé *"To your health,"* À la vôtre (response) *"And to yours"*
Frisia
Tsjoch
Georgia
Vakhtanguri, Gaumardschoss (to group of men),
Gagimardschoss (to single person)
Germany
For beer: Prost
For wine: Zum Wohl *"To your health"*
For cocktails: Auf uns *"To us"* or Auf Dich *"To you"*
For schnapps: Und weg *or* Hau' weg das Zeug *"Down the hatch,"* but Prost is fine as well.
For whisky: Cheers *or a toast like* Auf Schottland *"To Scotland"*
Hau weg den Scheiss (vulgar)

Greece
Eis Igian, Stin ijiasas, Jamas
Greenland
Kassutta *"Let our glasses meet,"* Imeqatigiitta *"Let's drink together"*
Hawaii
Okole maluna
Hungary
Kedves egeszsegere, Egészségedre (to one person) *"To your health,"* Egészségetekre (to a group) *"To your health"*
Iceland
Skál
India
A la sature
Indonesia (Bahasa)
Pro *or* Tos
Ireland (Gaelic)
Sláinte *"To your health"*
Iran (Baluchi)
Vashi
Ireland
Sláinte *"To your health,"* Guid forder *"Good luck"* in Ulster-Scots
Israel (Hebrew)
L'Chaim *"To life"*
Italy
Cin cin (formal), Salute (informal)
Japan
Kampai, Banzai
Kenya (Kikuyu)
Rathima andu atene, Hey is jambo
Korea
Chukbae, Kong gang ul wi ha yo
Latvia
Uz veselibu

Lebanon
Kesak (to one person), Keskun (to a group)
Lithuania
I sueikata, I sveikas
Macedonia
Na zdravje *"To your health"*
Malta
Cheers, Aviva (old fashioned)
Netherlands (Dutch)
Proost, Geluk, *or* Gezondheid *"To your health"*
("Any other expression in any language can be and will be used. As long as we can drink it will be OK")
New Zealand (Maori)
Kia Ora *"Hello, good health"*
Norway (Nynorsk)
Skål
Iran (Persian)
(Be) salam ati *"To your health,"* Nush *"Enjoy it, and let it be part of your body"*
Pakistan (Urdu)
Djam
Philippines (Tagalog)
Mabuhay *"Long life"*
Poland
Na zdrowie *"To your health,"* Vivat
Portugal
A sia saide, Rhaeto-Romanic, Viva, Noroc *"Good luck"*
Russia
Na zdorovje *"To your health"*
Scotland (Gaelic)
Slaandjivaa *"To your health,"* Slainte mhoiz
Slainte Mhath *"Good health"* Response: Slainte Mhor *"Great health"*
Here's tae ye

Senegal (Diola)
Buubuh, uhobal boh *"Here it is: let's drink"*
(Woolof) Niooko book *"It's ours"*
Serbia
Zivio Ziveli (pronounced 'zjee-ve-lee') *"Let's live long"*
Slovenia
Na zdravie *"To your health,"* Stolicka, Stolitschka
Somalia
Auguryo
South Africa (Afrikaans)
Gesondheid *"To your health"*
Spain (Catalan)
Salut, Txin txin,
Sant Hilari, Sant Hilari, fill de puta qui no se l'aCabi *"Son of a bitch the one that does not finish the cup"* (vulgar)
Spain (Galician)
Saúde
Spain (Spanish)
Salud, Chin chin
Arriba, abajo, al centro, para adentro *"Up, down, center, inside"* (vulgar)
Sweden
Skål, Skaal, Helan går *"Everything goes"*
Tanzania (Swahili)
Maisha marefu *"Good life"* or *"Cheers,"* Afya Vifijo
Thailand
Choc-tee, Hallo
Hey sawadekaa (to male) Hey sawadekap (to female)
Turkey
Şerefe *"To honor,"* Sağlığına (to one person) *"To your health,"* Sagliginiza (to a group, or polite) *"To your health"*
Turkistan (Uyghur)
Hoshe *"Cheers,"* Salametlikingiz ucun *"For your health"*

Ukraine
Budmo *"Shall we live forever"* (Everybody answers 'Hey'
Repeat three times, then everybody empties their glasses.
)
United Arab Emirates (Arabic)
Shucran, Fisehatak *"To your health"*
The Vatican (Latin)
Sanitas bona *"To your health,"* Bene tibi
Vietnam
Chia, Cạn chén (North V.N.) Cạn ly
Wales
Iechyd da
International Non-Places:
Esperanto
Je via sano *"To your health,"* Toston *"A toast"*
Interlingua
A vostre sanitate *"To your health,"* A vostre salute

TEST YOUR WI-Q
What does your wine drinking say about you?
And will it ever shut up?

A recent psychological study shows that your wine drinking
habits have a direct correlation with your personality. Take this
simple quiz to reveal your coping styles, or curl up with a loved-
one and take it together! First, find the statement below that
best describes your wine style. Then refer to Part Two to learn
what it says about you.

Part One: Questions

1. I drink slowly, savor every drop, and swirl each sip around
   my mouth to appreciate the full taste and aroma.
2. Bring me Champagne! Life is for celebrating!

215

3. My wine cellar is my pride. I've been collecting first growths since 1959.

4. Wine's first duty is to be red.

5. I prefer a sophisticated, dry white.

6. I usually order Merlot. It's soft, reliable, and I can pronounce it.

7. I often spend five minutes interrogating the sommelier and I'm not afraid to send wine back if it doesn't meet my standards.

8. I'm not one of those wine snobs. I drink white Zinfandel because I like it. So what?!

9. Exploring new wine I've never heard of is an adventure.

10. In this bag? Ripple, I think. I dunno. You got a dollar?

Part Two: Answers

1. You have a sensual, artistic nature; you relish every experience. In fact, everything you do takes way too long and you drive everyone crazy because you're never ready on time.

2. You're an exciting, carefree person, always the life of the party. You have a wide circle of friends. You have to because by the end of the party you've always made such an idiot of yourself that your old friends are embarrassed to be seen with you.

3. You are capable of deep feelings and form lasting emotional attachments. When you love someone you hang on like a leech and won't let go even when it's obvious to the rest of the world that their phone isn't broken, it's off the hook. You're a yawning black hole of neediness.

4. You have a Rabelaisian appetite for life. Dramatic music, spicy foods and bright colors attract you. You play your car stereo way too loud at traffic lights. You have an elevated sense of your own self-worth. You probably beat your wife.

5. You have highly developed organizational skills. Everything has to be color coordinated. If things don't go your way, you throw a hissy fit, sulk and ruin everyone else's night. You're a pain in the ass.

6. Your calmness and serenity make you invaluable in the workplace. In fact, you're the only one who's ever kept the tollbooth job for more than a month. Your children sometimes ask your wife who "that guy who lives here" is.

7. You have fine, discriminating tastes and great attention to detail. You check under your bed every night and sometimes hear voices. Medication might make the black helicopters go away.

8. Congratulations! You don't follow the pack! You live in your own little world of denial and don't notice the pathetic shambles you've made of your life. If you seek counseling now, it might not be too late.

9. You're a risk taker who sees the big picture. You're successful in business because your ruthless, cutthroat tendencies strangle the competition. You're selfish, greedy, and have no empathy for others.

10. You're practical and thrifty, and don't let the false promises of worldly possessions bog you down. You have a good chance of happiness in life.

Well, there you have it. I hope you were able to gain some valuable insight that will help you in your day-to-day interactions. And I also hope you get the treatment you need.

PRONUNCIATION GUIDE

Aglianico [ah-<u>lyah</u>-nee-ko]
Albariño [ahl-bah-<u>ree</u>-nyo]
Alicante [ahl-ee-<u>kahn</u>-teh]
Alsace [ahl-<u>zahs</u>]
Amarone [ah-mah-<u>ro</u>-neh]
Appellation d'Origine Controllée [ah-peh-lah-<u>syo(n)</u> do-hree-<u>zheen</u> ko(n)-tro-<u>lay</u>]
Apuglia [ah-<u>poo</u>-lee-ah]
Asti Spumante [<u>ahs</u>-tee spoo-<u>mahn</u>-teh]
Auslese [<u>aows</u>-lay-zeh]
Barbera d'Asti [bahr-<u>beh</u>-rah d<u>ahs</u>-tee]
Barolo [bah-<u>roh</u>-lo]
Batteria [baht-teh-<u>ree</u>-eh]
Beaujolais [bo-zho-<u>lay</u>]
Beaumes de Venise [bom duh vuh-<u>neez</u>]
Beaune [bone]
Beerenauslese [<u>bay</u>-rehn-<u>aows</u>-lay-zeh]
Bierzo [bee-<u>ehr</u>-tho]
Blanc de Blancs [bla(n) duh <u>bla(n)</u>]
Blanc de Noirs [bla(n) duh <u>nwahr</u>]
Bollinger [bo-lah(n)-<u>zhay</u>]
Bonarda [bo-n<u>ahr</u>-dah]
Bordeaux [bohr-<u>do</u>]
Bourboulenc [boohr-boo-<u>la(n)k</u>]
Bouteille [boo-<u>tay</u>]
Cabernet Franc [kah-behr-neh <u>fra(n)</u>]
Cabernet Sauvignon [kah-behr-neh so-vee-<u>nyo(n)</u>]
Cahors [kah-<u>ohr</u>]
Campania [kahm-<u>pah</u>-nyah]
Carmenère [kahr-muh-<u>nehr</u>]
Cava [<u>kah</u>-vah]
Chablis [shah-<u>blee</u>]
Château d'Yquem [sha-to dee-<u>kehm</u>]
Château Giraud [sha-to gee-<u>hro</u>]
Châteauneuf-du-Pape [shah-to-nuhf dew <u>pahp</u>]

Chenin Blanc [shuh-nah(n) bla(n)]
Chianti [kyahn-tee]
Clairette de Die [klay-hret duh dee]
Classico [klahs-see-ko]
Colli di Scandiano [kohl-lee dee skahn-dyah-no]
Condrieu [ko(n)-dryuh]
Cos d'Estournel [ko dehs-toohr-nehl]
Côte du Rhône [kot dew hron]
Côte Rôtie [kot ro-tee]
Crozes-Hermitage [kroz ehr-mee-tahzh]
Cserszegi Fűszeres [chehr-seggy few-sehr-ehj]
Darabbantartás [dor-rohb-bohn-tor-tahs]
Dégorgement [day-gohr-zhuh-ma(n)]
Denominazione d'Origine Controllata [deh-no-mee-nah-tsyo-ne dee o-ree-jee-neh con-trohl-lah-tah]
Dolcetto [dol-cheht-to]
Dosage [do-zah-zh]
Douro [do-roo]
Échézeaux [ay-shay-zo]
Einzellage [iyn-tsehl-lah-geh]
Eiswein [iys-viyn]
Erbaluce [ehr-bah-loo-cheh]
Eszencia [eh-sehn-see-ah]
Fiano [fee-ah-no]
Friuli [free-oo-lee]
Frizzante [freets-sahn-teh]
Gamay [gah-may]
Garnacha [gahr-nah-chah]
Gewürztraminer [gay-vewrts-trah-mee-neh(r)]
Gran Reserva [grahn reh-sehr-bah]
Grand Cru Classé [gra(n) khrew klah-say]
Grappa [grahp-pah]
Graves [ghrahv]
Greco del Tufo [greh-ko dee too-fo]
Grenache [ghruh-nahsh]
Grosslage [gros-lah-geh]
Grüner Veltliner [ghrew-neh(r) fehlt-lee-neh(r)]

Hermitage [ehr-mee-tahzh]
Lafite Rothschild [lah-feet hrot-sheeld]
Lagrein [lah-grayn]
Languedoc-Roussillon [la(n)-guh-dok hroo-see-yo(n)]
Latour [lah-toohr]
Laurent-Perrier [lo-hra(n) peh-ryay]
Loire [lwahr]
Malbec [mahl-behk]
Marches [mahr-keh]
Marsanne [mar-sahn]
Melon de Bourgogne [muh-lo(n) duh boohr-go-nyeh]
Merlot [mehr-lo]
Meursault-Charmes [muhr-so shahrm]
Mevushal [meh-voo-shahl]
Michel Chapoutier [mee-shehl shah-poo-tyay]
Monastrell [mo-nahs-trehl]
Montello Rosso [mon-teh-lo ros-so]
Montsant [mohn-sahnt]
Moscato d'Asti [mos-kah-to dahs-tee]
Mourvèdre [moohr-vehdr]
Moussant [moo-sah(n)]
Mouton Rothschild [moo-to(n) hrot-sheeld]
Muscadelle [mews-kah-dehl]
Muscadet [mews-kah-deh]
Muscat de Frontignan [mews-kah duh fro(n)-teen-nya(n)]
Muscatel [mews-kah-tehl]
Muskateller [m(oo)s-kah-tehl-leh(r)]
Nero d'Avola [neh-ro dah-vo-lah]
Nicolas Joly [nee-ko-las zho-lee]
Nouveau [noo-vo]
Nuit St. Georges [nwee sah(n) zhorzh]
Petit Verdot [puh-tee vehr-do]
Pétrus [pay-trews]
Picpoul de Pinet [peek-pool duh pee-neh]
Pineau d'Aunis [pee-no do-nee]
Pinot Blanc [pee-no bla(n)]
Pinot Grigio [pee-no gree-jo]

Pinot Gris [pee-no ghree]
Pinot Noir [pee-no nwahr]
Pinotage [pee-no-tahj]
Piper-Heidsieck [pee-pehr hayd-zeek]
Pouilly-Fuissé [poo-yee fwee-say]
Pouilly-Fumé [poo-yee few-may]
Prädikat [preh-dee-kaht]
Primitivo [pree-mee-tee-vo]
Priorato [pree-o-rah-to]
Prosecco [pro-zehk-ko]
Puttonyo [poo-tohn-yo]
Qualitätswein mit Prädikat [kvah-lee-tayts-viyn mit preh-dee-kaht]
Reserva [reh-sehr-bah]
Retour de l'Inde [hre-toohr duh land]
Rhein [hriyn]
Rhône [hron]
Rias Baixas [ree-ahs bah-ee-sahs]
Riesling [hrees-ling]
Rioja [ree-o-hah]
Riserva [ree-sehr-vah]
Romanée Conti [hro-mah-nay ko(n)-tee]
Rueda [roo-eh-dah]
Sagrentino [sah-grahn-tee-no]
Saignée [sahy-nyay]
Sancerre [sa(n)-sehr]
Sangiovese di Romagna [sahn-jo-veh-zeh dee ro-mah-nyah]
Sangria Blanca [sahn-gree-ah blahn-kah]
Sauternes [so-tehrn]
Sauvignon Blanc [so-vee-nyo(n) bla(n)]
Savigny-lès-Beaune [sah-vee-nyee lay bon]
Scheurebe [shoy-ray-beh]
Sekt [zehkt]
Sélection de Grains Nobles [say-lehk-syo(n) duh ghrah(n) nobl]
Sémillon [say-mee-yo(n)]
Sèvre et Maine [sehvr ay mayn]

221

Silvaner [zil-vah-neh(r)]
Solera [so-leh-ra]
Spätlese [shpayt-lay-zeh]
Spumante [spoo-mahn-teh]
St. Emilion [sah(n) tay-mee-lyo(n)]
Tannat [tah-nah]
Tempranillo [tehm-prah-nee-yo]
Terroir [teh-hrwahr]
Tocai Friulano [to-kah-ee free-oo-lah-no]
Tokaj [to-kah-ee]
Tokaj-Hegyalja [to-kah-ee hed-jyah-lya]
Tokaji Aszú [tokah-ee ah-zoo]
Torrontés [to-ron-tehs]
Trebbiano [trehb-byah-no]
Trentino-Alto Adige [trehn-tee-no ahl-to ah-dee-jeh]
Trocken [trohk-kehn]
Trockenbeerenauslese [trohk-kehn-bay-rehn-aows-lay-zeh]
Ullage [uh-ledge]
Vendange Tardive [va(n)-da(n)-zh tahr-deev]
Veneto [veh-neh-to]
Verdejo [behr-deh-ho]
Verdicchio dei Castelli di Jesi [vehr-deek-kyo day kahs-tehl-lee dee yeh-zee]
Vermentino [vehr-mehn-tee-no]
Vernaccia di San Gimignano [vehr-naht-chah dee sahn jee-mee-nyah-no]
Vigneron [vee-nyuh-hro(n)]
Vin de Pays [vah(n) duh peh-yee]
Vinho Verde [vee-nyoo vehr-dee]
Vinos de Denominación de Origen Calificada [bee-nos deh deh-no-mee-nah-thee-on deh o-ree-hehn kah-lee-fee-kah-dah]
Viognier [vyo-nyay]
Viura [bee-oo-rah]
Vouvray [voo-vhray]
Yecla [yeh-klah]

About the Author

Winner of the 2005 James Beard Award for Internet writing, Jennifer Rosen writes the weekly wine column for the Rocky Mountain News and contributes to other publications around the world. Her first book, *Waiter, There's a Horse in My Wine*, won the 2005 Gourmand World Cookbook Award for Wine Literature. Her internet newsletter goes out to 40,000 readers around the globe.

A sought-after wine educator and entertainer, her seminar topics range from *Secrets of Blind Tasting* to *Wine & Sex*. Jennifer lives in Denver, CO, and travels frequently to wine regions around the world, where she speaks French and Italian, stutters Spanish and German and has begun destroying Arabic. She is certified as a ski instructor, horse trainer, and handwriting analyst, and works off the job perks with belly dance and trapeze.

jester@corkjester.com   www.corkjester.com